THE GENDER TRAP

BOOK 1: Education and Work
BOOK 2: Sex and Marriage
BOOK 3: Messages and Images

THE GENDER TRAP is a series of books about the sex roles imposed on girls and boys in our society, written for young people in school, college and at work, and for their teachers and parents.

Book 3: *MESSAGES AND IMAGES*, looks at language and the way we use words and images in jokes, cartoons, picture postcards, pop lyrics, books and films, showing how this underlines and sometimes creates stereotypes. Values created by advertising, newspapers and magazines, and the beauty business are discussed, showing how artificial and demanding these values can be for both men and women. Hard facts and provocative questions encourage girls and boys to see how rigid ideas about their roles can restrict the lives and experiences of both sexes.

Book 1: *EDUCATION AND WORK*, and Book 2: *SEX AND MARRIAGE*, complete the series - all are published in hard and paperback editions. Each book includes cartoons, poems, stories, extracts, interviews, questions and ideas for projects, discussion and debate. *THE GENDER TRAP* is both an essential handbook for use in schools and colleges and a comprehensive introduction to these crucial issues for the general public.

Carol Adams and Rae Laurikietis are both in their mid-twenties, and both are history graduates. They teach history/social studies and English respectively at a London comprehensive school.

BOOK 3: MESSAGES AND IMAGES

THE
GENDER
TRAP

A CLOSER LOOK AT SEX ROLES

Carol Adams & Rae Laurikietis

Cartoons by Andy Johnson

Revised for American Readers
by Jill Dunnell Sellers

First published in London by VIRAGO Ltd 1976
in association with Quartet Books Ltd

VIRAGO is a feminist publishing imprint: 'It is only when women start to organize in large numbers that we become a political force, and begin to move towards the possibility of a truly democratic society in which every human being can be brave, responsible, thinking and diligent in the struggle to live at once freely and unselfishly.'

SHEILA ROWBOTHAM, *Women, Resistance and Revolution*

Revised American Edition published by Academy Press, Limited 1977

Adams, Carol.
    The gender trap.

    Includes bibliographies.
    CONTENTS: Book 1. Education and work. — Book 2. Sex and marriage. — Book 3. Messages and images.
    1. Young adults — Collected works. 2. Sex role — Collected works. 3. Sex discrimination — Collected works.
4. Sex instruction for youth — Collected works.
5. Marriage — Collected works. 6. Social values — Collected works. I. Laurikietis, Rae, joint author.
II. Title.
HQ799.5.A3   1977   301.41   77-22605
ISBN 0-915864-13-4 pbk.
ISBN 0-915864-30-4 lib. bdg.

CONTENTS

AUTHOR'S NOTE

In the last few years the subject of 'Women's Liberation' has become a major issue. People ask what it is that women want liberating from, and how this liberation will affect the future of both women and men.

This series of books, intended for young people in schools, colleges and at work, and their parents and teachers attempts to answer some of the many questions behind these larger ones. What emerges is that Women's Liberation is not a cause for the benefit of women only: rather, it is part of a larger movement which asks both men and women to question their accepted roles in society.

The last book in this series examines our language, humor and the media that surround us in our everyday lives, looking especially at some of the stereotypes we are influenced by. Certain areas that particularly concern women, such as cosmetics and fashion, are examined in detail.

The first book in this series, *EDUCATION AND WORK*, looks at how children are brought up and educated, and at the world of housework, work and trade unions. The second book, *SEX AND MARRIAGE,* examines the relationship between the sexes, love, marriage and the family.

As a whole *THE GENDER TRAP* shows the injustice and restrictions of a society that programs its men and women to lead separate and different lives according to stereotypes and suggests that things could be different.

C.A. and R.L.

ACKNOWLEDGEMENTS

We should like to thank the following for permission to quote from their songs: 'A Little Piece of Leather' reproduced by kind permission of April Music Ltd, words and music by Donnie Albert; 'Sugar Sugar' reproduced by kind permission of Kirshner/Warner Bros. Music Ltd; 'She's A Teaser' written by Vic Malcolm, published by Red Bus Music (International) Ltd, reproduced by kind permission of Red Bus Music (International) Ltd; 'Little Town Flirt' reproduced by kind permission of Vicki Music Ltd and Carlin Music Corp.; 'Hang On In There Baby' reproduced by kind permission of Warner Bros. Music Ltd; 'Bobby's Girl' by Kassner Assoc. Publishers Ltd; 'Don't Let Him Touch You' copyright 1971 Jonjo Music Co. Ltd; and Astra for her poem.

PART ONE:

IT'S NO JOKE

PART ONE:

13

1
HAVE YOU HEARD THE JOKE ABOUT THE . . .

Much of what we find funny in jokes and cartoons relies for its effect on our recognition of the peculiarities of male and female behavior. Women are supposed to behave in a way that is 'typical' of their sex and so are men; all mothers-in-law are supposed to nag and all young men are supposed to be horny. We have so absorbed these stereotypes into our views that the jokes would not be funny if their characters didn't behave in this way.

So, you might ask, what's wrong with a good joke about courting couples, for example? Like jokes about 'hillbillies,' Jews and Poles, they may reinforce misleading and crude ideas about what people are like and how they behave. Jokes are OK if the people they portray are somehow seen as equal, but they're often another way of presenting men and women as different and at odds with each other. This is not so funny in real life. First of all we'll look at the image of women in jokes and cartoons. They tend to fall into certain stereotypes.

'The Old Lady' — the Missis

The nagging wife is not the most attractive of women to look at. She often wears curlers and has a cigarette butt hanging from the corner of her mouth. Her clothes are dowdy and she always carries a large bag. Her role is to hen-peck and to dominate the life of her husband, and the expression on her face shows this. We wonder why he has had the misfortune to get lumbered with her.

The Missis stereotype is Andy Capp's wife, Flo. We know just what to expect of her. She won't let the man out of her sight, takes charge of the money and rations him his portion to go down to the corner bar. She's continually suspicious of what he's up to with the barmaid, and is ready with the rolling pin when he returns home. If she's not out working she's in the house waiting on her husband or doing housework. He, of course, has his faults, like getting drunk, gambling, being lazy and disorganized — all of which she tries to change. This is what makes her so objectionable.

There is a variation on the theme of the Missis, and that is the Upper-class Wife, like Lady Plushbottom in the Moon Mullins comics. She is equally unattractive, always wears a hat, has a sharp upturned face and always looks down her nose. She may be shown discovering her husband on the sofa with the maid, and perhaps telling her friends that it's the only way they can get servants nowadays. Like the working-class wife, there is never any chance of her going off with somebody else. She marches into shops and makes ridiculous demands on amazed shopkeepers. She's a total snob — in a way that men in jokes rarely are.

Some examples

Flo — 'Your breakfast's getting cold.'
Andy — 'Won't be a sec, I'm looking over the racing form.'
Andy is not reading the paper but gazing out of the window.
'Yes, that little darlin' next door gets later every morning.'

Friend calls for Andy — 'Opening time.'
Andy — 'Not today Charlie, I'm staying in with Florrie.'
Friend — 'You didn't come down yesterday either — what's this strange hold she has over you?'
Andy — 'It's a cross between a single leg Boston an' a single side head lock.'

Oh no, not the Mother-in-law

Closely related to the Missis is the Mother-in-law. She is a favorite topic for jokes. She's always the wife's mother, so she has all the worst qualities of the nagging wife, plus the fact that she is an interfering outsider. She arrives unexpectedly to stay and makes life a misery when there, ganging up with the wife against the poor victimized husband. Her visits mean the end of peace, privacy or relaxation. She is completely sexless, she often seems to have been widowed since time immemorial, and we can hardly imagine her married with children. Probably she drove the poor father-in-law to his grave, or away, long ago. She seems to have little life of her own, and is always on the phone to the wife offering old-fashioned advice on how to bring up the children or deal with the husband.

Some examples

Andy — 'I met yer mother in the pub pet, I saw her alright for booze.'
Flo — 'That was very sweet of yer pet.'
Andy — 'It was nothin'. She's so tight lipped, half a pint lasts her all evenin'.'

Heard in the bar of a London hotel (middle-aged American to friend) — 'Don't talk to me about the Trevi fountain in Rome! I threw all my loose change in it and made a wish, but the wife's mother was still at the hotel when I got back.'

And as one judge said, the maximum penalty for bigamy is having two mothers-in-law!

'If you say so dear' — the Scatterbrain

Next in the lineup of funny females is the scatterbrain. Sometimes she's young, blonde and reasonably all right to look at. But that's about all that can be said for her. She doesn't have a single brain in her pretty head — she's the bird-brained dim-wit, usually somebody's wife, like Blondie Bumstead. But she can be single, like Lolly in the comic strip, with a girl friend who sets her off, like Lolly's overweight, ridiculous 'women's lib' office buddy. One of the scatterbrain's main characteristics is that she can't handle money. She can't even add, so her boyfriend's or husband's life is plagued by endless bills, the result of her extravagance with clothes and her general lack of skill in household management. She is useless with gadgets and likely to maim herself for life opening a tin can. One species of scatterbrain is the woman driver; she regularly smashes up the car and it's a wonder she's allowed on the open road.

More often today the scatterbrain is an older woman, like Edith Bunker in 'All In The Family'. She features in endless jokes about women and money, women needing a man around the house and women's stupidity. She always misses the point of a joke, and when she tries to solve any problem she creates a hundred more. She may sometimes try to be romantic and get her husband to remember the days when they were courting. But her husband finds her affection and concern foolish or embarassing.

Some examples

Wife — 'Well, I've worked out our budget for this week. I've added up the figures ten times.'
Husband — 'That's the way to do it doll, you've got to be thorough.'
Wife — 'Yes. Trouble is I don't know which of the ten answers is right.'

Woman comes in from parking the family car in the garage. Her husband looks up apprehensively. She says — 'Nothing exciting — just the usual bumps and a few scratches.'

'Well, there was this Blonde ...'

Immediately recognizable by her sexy figure, the dumb blonde often says nothing at all, although she is the most common character in popular dirty jokes. All the teller of the joke has to do to show who he's talking about is to draw the outline of her hourglass figure with his hands. She is found in the television series "Love American Style" and in movies with Marilyn Monroe or Elke Sommers.

18

In this type of joke all men are after is a bit of sex. Wizened old professors and portly bank managers drool over their desks at the sight of her cleavage. She manages to appear in the middle of a football team photo as the mascot. She's the babysitter who entices the innocent husband into the broom closet; she's the patient who ensnares the doctor on his examination table; she's the over-developed schoolgirl who gives the boys practical lessons in experimental biology. It is from her that the nagging wives are protecting their men.

Some examples

Real Estate Office: man behind the desk; blonde with cleavage enters — 'Do you mind sharing with me if I can get the old woman to move out?'

Have you heard the joke about the filmstar Busty Bertha — 72-32-36.
Question — 'What can she actually do?'
Answer — 'With a little help she can actually sit down.'

Wild Thing — the Amazon

She's more of a fantasy than a joke. She is superwoman, tall, dark and sexy, usually wearing a skimpy leather jerkin outfit and long black boots. She has a hard cat-like face with wild eyes and a cruel mouth. She doesn't exist in the cozy world of other women. Her world is one of adventure with men; spying, travelling to other planets, the criminal underworld. She doesn't portray women in real life at all, but the women of men's fantasies; wild, untameable, and a challenge. She is found in James Bond-style films with her whip and a gun at her hips. She is Modesty Blaise and Barbarella.

This woman is a figure of fun in a peculiar way because she represents everything women aren't (but men are) allowed to be. Dressed as she is, and found in the most incredible situations, she seems ridiculous.

What characteristics do the men have in the cartoons we have mentioned, e.g. Andy Capp? Are they at all a true reflection of what men are like?

Why are there no jokes about fathers-in-law?

Are women in jokes ever lazy and irresponsible?

Are men ever stupid and dumb?

Do any of the people you know remotely resemble the types we have discussed?

Notice that men in jokes are usually incompetent around the house and can't change a diaper to save their lives. Do you think these ideas will still be funny to future generations who see men and women as having less separate roles?

Try reversing the roles of men and women in jokes. Are they still funny?

2
'A LOVELY PAIR'
POSTCARDS AND
GREETING CARDS

One form of humor that most people agree is funny, if a bit vulgar, are postcards and greeting cards in which men and women are caricatured to the extreme. Certain ideas keep repeating themselves in various ways. Women have outsized breasts and hips, mostly exposed, which are supposed to make them attractive. But their very noticeable charms give rise to 'funny' situations:

A postcard showing a girl on the beach eating a pear — a passing stranger stops in his tracks to comment, 'Wow, what a great pair!' It's obvious he is not talking about what she is eating, but about her size 40 breasts.

A greeting card showing a shapely girl, her skirt lifted by the wind to show her legs, underwear, and garters — captioned: 'I think you should know what people are saying behind your back'. Inside — 'WOW!'

If women are not shown to be outrageously exaggerated sex objects, then they are shown as either fat and ugly or thin and ugly. One going-away card shows an impossibly dumpy stewardess, and calls her 'your flight bag'. If the ugly woman is married, her husband gets all the sympathy. On one postcard two couples are shown. Of one couple the wife is grossly overweight, her husband pathetically thin. The other couple comment:

'He's joined a wife-swapping group.'
'Brother, I don't blame him.'

Why no jokes about husband-swapping groups?

Another well worn myth that figures in the postcard centers around the horny male — who could be a window-cleaner or a milkman. His women customers are sexually easy game. They are home all day, alone in the house with little to do. A typical situation involves a young housewife, shown in revealing underwear. Housewife (wearing negligee) in the living room —

'Uh-oh, here comes my husband. Can you come back tonight?'
Milkman — 'What, on my own time? Are you kidding, lady?'

For the milkman, sex with his female customers is part of the job, one of the benefits, not something he has to go out of his way for, or dress up for. The businessman has his benefits, too, according to one card that says: 'Congratulations on your promotion! You are now entitled to go skinny-dipping in the secretarial pool'.

Another thing that is likely to strike you as you see these postcards is the unbelievable naivete of the women. They:

(a) wear clothes that would normally get them arrested for indecent exposure, or at least for disturbing the peace. If they're young and attractive the only thing that could possibly be on their minds is men;
(b) make innocent but suggestive remarks without appearing to realize what they've said, which the man immediately interprets as sexual. A favorite one is the housewife at the grocer's saying 'I want stuffing, please';
(c) show everything they've got without realizing it. The men wear expressions of varying degrees of ecstasy at the sight. The women themselves don't have any idea, of course, of the effect they're having;
(d) are always having things done to them. They're on the receiving end. They are sex objects all right, just waiting to be handled. For example, two bathing beauties in their bikinis are looking at an octopus in the acquarium. The blonde says to her friend — 'This reminds me, Jack is dating me tonight.' The men on the other hand, are shown to have only one interest in women — a sexual one. They're also supposed to go to any length to 'get a piece'.

So next time somebody sends you a postcard, look at it carefully.

We've discussed the jokes about women's breasts — the bigger the better. Notice how the same applies to jokes about men's sexual organs.

Think of any postcards that you found funny. Why were they funny?

24

3
LANGUAGE

It's an insult

The language we use expresses the way we experience the world around us, and the words people use in talking about men and women reveal their attitudes towards them. One particularly good example of this is the way words with sexual overtones are used. If the list of sexually insulting words were divided into two, one for women and one for men, the women's would be far, far longer. Even when words are meant to insult men, they either reflect back on women, or are used in an almost complimentary fashion.

Let's take a closer look at the insults and sexually loaded words directed at men. One that comes to mind is 'bastard', which originally meant to be born illegitimately. If a child is born a bastard then, by implication, it is the mother who is to blame. It is she who 'got into trouble'. But often the word is not used as a deliberate insult but in an admiring sense, such as 'Girls go for men who are bastards', or 'He can be a real bastard when he wants to be', meaning he is tough and ruthless — characteristics admired in men, as stereotypes.

Other insults directed at men, such as 'son-of-a bitch', get at men by slandering the women they're closest to, in the same way that the expression 'mamma's boy' does. Another expression, the 'hen-pecked' man, reflects on his wife.

But you insult a woman very simply. You don't implicate her father, her husband, her brother or any other man. You merely suggest she is a prostitute. The vast majority of sexual insults aimed at women are derived from prostitution or women's sexuality. For example:

hooker	piece	broad	fancy woman
whore	tart	callgirl	streetwalker
trollop	harlot	slut	bitch
tramp	floozy	bag	hustler

You wouldn't be able to find so many words that refer to men who *use* prostitutes. There are very few, and they're mainly the names of men who control prostitutes, e.g. 'pimp'.

But the surprising thing is just how often you hear these words and expressions used in the most ordinary situations. What is even more surprising is how often women use these words themselves about each other, without realizing the extent to which this shows contempt for all women. Both sexes have absorbed an attitude to women's sexuality that is one of disapproval and sometimes contempt.

There are certain words in pairs that have a sexual association for the feminine word while the masculine word has a respectable, businesslike meaning. For example, 'sir' and 'madam'. When you call man 'sir' it conveys respect. But the word 'madam' has also come to mean a woman who runs a brothel. The words 'master' and 'mistress' are similar. Master implies having control and can mean the head of a household, the owner of animals, a position of importance. Master is used in such compound words as masterpiece, masterplan, mastermind, master-craftsman. The word mistress, on the other hand, in addition to its usual meaning has acquired a sexual connotation — that of a woman having intercourse with a man she isn't married to.

Similarly, being a call-boy is perfectly respectable. It simply refers to a person who calls actors when it is time for them to go on stage. But being a call-girl is an entirely different matter. It means a prostitute. Then there is showman and showgirl, and many others.

Take the words host and hostess. A host is a man who entertains or gives shelter to a guest or visitor. A hostess, though commonly used to describe a woman entertaining a home, can also be a polite way of saying 'prostitute'.

Similarly, when you call a man a tramp, even though that is not particularly flattering, you are describing his way of life. But to call a woman a tramp is to condemn her sexual morals.

When you call a man an honest man you mean that his honesty and integrity can't be questioned. But when you refer to a woman as an honest woman, you are referring to her sexuality, implying that she is sexually pure or faithful.

When you want to be insulting what words do you use? Do you use different words for the two sexes?

The diminutive

There are in our language several pairs of words that show the more powerful role of the male, and the female as less important. One way this distinction is made is by adding 'ess' or 'ette' to the end of the masculine word. These are diminutive endings and usually indicate something little or smaller. Compare the following lists:

major	majorette
usher	usherette
governor	governess
adventurer	adventuress

Where there are masculine and feminine nouns, the meanings of the feminine ones have usually undergone a subtle change for the worse. Look at this list:

king	queen
brave	squaw
wizard	witch
landlord	landlady
patron	matron
grandfatherly advice	old wives' tales

27

To show what we mean, the word 'landlord' has the ring of ownership and possessions, while 'landlady' is not quite so grand. She is more of a housekeeper who imposes petty restrictions.

Compare how the words king and queen are used. King is the more powerful. In advertising it is used to suggest size — something big, the best you can get. So you sell an expensive brand of cigarettes by calling them king-sized. Size is only another indication of power. This is not so when the word queen is used. Usually it is applied to what is basically trivial. There are May queens, beauty queens, Post Office Machinery queens. And if the word is not used trivially it is used in a rather offensive way about a homosexual man.

The word 'man' itself is used to convey the idea of power and size. Man-sized tissues are larger and stronger than feminine tissues, which are pastel-colored, perfumed and fragile. We hear the words *man*power, chair*man,* sports*man*ship used often when it is women we are talking about. How many more can you think of?

There are some roles in life that women are assumed to take unless you make it clear that in this particular case you are talking about a man. Because prostitutes and models are thought of as women, you have to say male prostitute and male model to show you are talking about a man. Marriage is supposed to be a more important event for women than for men, so the word bride appears in words like bridesmaid, bridal gown, bridal attendant, and even bridegroom. But the word groom does not appear in any of the words to do with weddings except for bridegroom. When a marriage ends in divorce, the woman becomes a divorcee. That is her change of title, but for the man you have to make the statement that 'he is divorced'.

Take a word pair like manager and manageress, and think of all ways in which you would use them. Are there any differences? If so, what are they?

Women as ...

... An Endless buffet

The idea that women are passive creatures is reflected in the language we use about them when we are being complimentary as well as abusive. The words we use can identify women with plants and animals, but the most passive of them are connected with food. What can be more lifeless and passive than a plate of food? Women are:

> Honey
> sugar
> cheesecake
> sweetie pies

They have cherry lips and peaches-and-cream complexions. They look delicious, like delectable morsels, they look 'good enough to eat'. Even as a compliment, the food they are

compared with is different, delightful perhaps, but somehow frivolous, whereas men are described as beefcake, or hunks of meat — much more substantial.
Women are described as being:

a dish
a tasty bit
a sweet young thing
a juicy piece
luscious
ripe
fresh
hot
crumpet

. . . 'Nice bit of crumpet'

In an interview with the English disc-jockey Jimmy Savile which appeared in a national newspaper, Jimmy talked at length about the 'crumpet' he has had — and he wasn't talking about the sort you eat:

'Jimmy says that it is great to be famous. There are cars and caravans and houses and flats. And crumpet. Jimmy is canny about talking of his crumpet. In AS IT HAPPENS [his autobiography] he says that there have been incidents on trains and boats and planes and bushes and fields, corridors, doorways, floors, chairs, slag heaps, desks, and probably everything except the celebrated chandelier and ironing board. But you never see Jimmy's love life plastered across the newspapers.'

Another example from a newspaper:

'. . . Sir John Spleen drew attention to the recent report that at the moment more boys are being born than girls. "This can only mean," he said, "that in the future, and not in some far-off future, but in our own lifetimes, we are going to be confronted with a serious shortage of crumpet. What is the Government doing about it? Nothing. How long, I ask you, can we afford to just sit back and idly let events take their course?" '

Just try reversing the situation, and imagine reading about famous women talking about the hot dogs they've had, or reading headlines about the coming hot dog shortage, or hearing one woman ask another where she can get a bit of hot dog. Perhaps it would be funnier if it were not so one-sided.

. . . Human zoo

Which column of words is usually applied to women?

stud	kitten	bitch
wolf	bunny	shrew
buck	bird	cow
lion-hearted	chick	nag
fox	lamb	sow

Even when men and women are compared with animals there is a distinction. Men are powerful, virile and aggressive animals. Women are either the pets, the domestic, tame, harmless, cuddly creatures, or are referred to by words that have acquired an unattractive flavor, such as those in the right-hand column above.

Notice how often the unflattering expressions are derived from the female rather than the male animal. A goose, the female, is a silly person. A cat is a malicious woman, especially prone to making unkind (catty) remarks about other women. A tomcat is something else altogether — sexually aggressive, without inhibitions.

31

... Shrinking violet

The fact that women are closely connected with plants also reinforces the idea that they are passive. When you deflower a woman you take away her virginity. At a dance or party you feel sorry for the girl who is a wallflower. A girl can also be described as a clinging vine, unable to think or act for herself, or a shrinking violet, over-fearful and timid. One well-known song even compares a girl with poison ivy!

Men are too active to be thought of as plants. There is one exception, however. When we want to be insulting we call a man a pansy, meaning, once again, a homosexual.

Even many of the names girls are given have their origin in plants, such as Lily, Daisy and Rose. Can you think of any names for men that come from plants? The names we give children often show the contrast we make between the two sexes and the different characteristics girls and boys are supposed to have:

Alexander — defender of men	Agnes — chaste
Arnold — eagle strength	Amanda — lovable
Barry — spear	Dinah — dedicated
Bernard — bear hand	Dolores — sorrows
Charles — manly	Fiona — fair
Ernest — resolute fighter	Gwyneth — blessed
Henry — house ruler	Margaret — pearl
Lionel — young lion	Miranda — to be admired
Martin — warlike	Rosalind — fair rose
Victor — conqueror	Stella — star

Virtues like faith, hope, charity, patience, joy and modesty are all girls' names. So are the months of the year, precious stones, rubies and pearls. Girls can be given boys' names such as Jo, Terry, Kelly, Chris, Pat and Toni. That is perfectly all right, in the same way that a girl can be called a tomboy. But it's less common for a boy to be given a girl's name — there's no acceptable equivalent of a 'tomboy' for a boy.

Him and Hers, Hers and His

He
She
It

in order of importance?

The superiority of men over women is reflected in the grammar of our language. A good example of this is the way in which the personal pronoun is used. He is used, not only to mean he, but also to mean he *and/or* she. This applies even when there is only a theoretical possibility that there is a man present. It may sound strange to an audience that is largely women to be referred to as 'he' but this is what usually happens. If you said 'she', any male present would feel immediately excluded.

It is often argued that 'he', meaning men and women, does not exclude women. In that case why not use 'she', as it combines both words very neatly? Perhaps we could come to use the word 'woman' when we mean both men and women, as this too contains both words. Or even 'people' or 'human beings', and leave 'man' to be used when we mean exclusively men.

Only a woman could be:

a battle-axe	an old bag
a gossip	a bathing beauty
hysterical	a flirt

There is no logical reason why these expressions could not be used when talking about men. Yet people immediately think of them as being exclusively descriptive of women. Try asking your friends.

How they say it

We've looked at how words themselves are used. There are also differences in the actual speech of men and women. Certain words and phrases are used mainly by men. They tend to be exclamations of various kinds, swear words and expressions that are taboo for women. Swearing is much more acceptable in a man than in a woman. For women it is at best 'not nice' and at worst shocking and disgusting.

Men are also conscious of not using 'bad' language when there is a 'lady' present. Women are brought up to use 'polite' language, to be correct in their speech, and often they seem to take greater care not to make grammatical errors — particularly if they want to appear to have status.

Where there is a local way of pronouncing a word, which differs from the 'proper' way, then it's often boys who are more likely to use it than girls. Working-class speech is associated with toughness, and toughness is generally considered to be desirable only for men. As women aren't expected to be tough, they're less likely to speak in a rough way than men.

Double talk

I find my husband has two separate vocabularies. If I talk to the woman next door I'm 'gossiping', but if he talks to her husband he's 'discussing things'; if I close my eyes while sitting in the easy chair, I'm 'dozing off'; when he does the same thing he's 'contemplating'; when I'm silent I'm 'moody', whereas he, of course, is 'being thoughtful'.

letter in a women's magazine

If you're a boy, do you ever consciously 'talk tough'?
If you're a girl, do you try to 'talk properly'?

4
THE MUSIC YOU HEAR

If you think of the words of some current pop songs, and of old ones for that matter, what sort of picture do you get of women? If the words of the songs are anything to go by, women are dumb, passive and childish.

SHE'S A LITTLE PIECE OF LEATHER

'And she's well put together-oo
She's the apple of my eye
She is my sweetie pie-oo
She is my cupcake, don't you make no mistake.'

April Music Ltd

SUGAR, SUGAR
'You are my candy girl
And I can't stop wanting you.'

Kirshner/Warner Bros. Music Ltd

On the other hand, when women in songs are freer, tougher, they're also often seen as untrustworthy, fickle and liable to run off with another man at any time. They're temptation for men, but, it seems, incapable of real loyalty. They really enjoy enticing men with their sexual wiles but they don't feel anything deeper:

SHE'S A TEASER

'She's got them big red lips, she's got shaking hips,
She's got flashing eyes that hypnotize.
She's got a clinging dress but she never says yes ...
She's a teaser, she's a teaser ...
You know she moves like a snake
But she's just a big fake ...'
                                    Red Bus Music (International) Ltd

LITTLE TOWN FLIRT

'You can get hurt, fooling around
With that little town flirt ...'
                                    Vicki Music Ltd and Carlin Music Corp.

Although there are some gentle songs for men, where they're genuinely involved with a girl, in many the implication is that all men want from women is sex:

HANG ON IN THERE BABY

'I'm gonna give you more than you ever dreamed possible.
Don't be afraid baby, oh no,
Sweet virgin of the world ...'
                                    Warner Bros Music Ltd

Some songs, particularly those of the Rolling Stones, are so sexually aggressive that they insult and put women down, and women themselves are conditioned to such an extent that many like these songs — in fact go wild over them. Consider some of the titles: Honky Tonk Woman, Back Street Girl, Look at That Stupid Girl, Yesterday's Girls, Under My Thumb.

Songs sung by women are usually along different lines. They are about 'real' love and often mention marriage:

36

37

I WANNA BE BOBBY'S GIRL

'That's the most important thing for me
And if I were Bobby's girl, if I were Bobby's girl
What a grateful thankful girl I'd be . . .'

                                        Kassner Assoc. Publishers Ltd

The men women sing about, and the men who sing about themselves, are true to stereotype — they're not to be trusted, they don't want to be tied down, they are the independent men who won't be trapped by love.

DON'T LET HIM TOUCH YOU

'He's playing the game of love and he's trying to
See how much you'll let him have.
And if he has you he will run away and leave you . . .'

                                        © Copyright 1971 Jonjo Music Co. Ltd

Does anything we have said apply to the latest hit single you bought?
Try listening to some records of this kind — those by the Rolling Stones in particular.
Does it matter what the words of pop songs say? Do they affect your ideas and feelings?

5
THE BOOKS YOU READ

In the first book in this series we looked at how school reading programs and the books young children read put over stereotyped ideas about men and women and the range of opportunities in their lives. It's important that we look at books for older children and adults to see whether this applies here too. In this section we're going to look at non-fiction and fiction, mainly the latter.

What did you do in the War, Mom?

Books on subjects such as history, psychology, art, sociology, philosophy and music reflect the position of women in society in a number of ways. On the whole these subjects are thought of as male territory — both the writers and those written about. Of course there are some exceptions — but what is most striking in the field of non-fiction is what is left *unsaid* by or about women.

History is a good example. History books give the impression often that only *men* make what is called history; that only the masculine fields of war, government and kings are 'real' history. The women who appear in most history books are the exceptional women — Joan of Arc, Boadicea (military leaders), Cleopatra, Nell Gwynn (sex bombs), Queen Victoria (royalty). One trouble is that history itself has for a long time been *defined* as being about certain kinds of events, and it's only recently that people have begun to be taught the history of how ordinary people lived — their ideas, daily lives, brave, cowardly and sad moments. Working-class history is beginning to be more widely written about and studied — as is the history of women.

Ordinary women came even lower down the scale of historical importance than ordinary men: their lives, when they were documented, were often recounted by men. There are exceptions: for example, in 1930 Ivy Pinchbeck wrote a book called *Women Workers and the Industrial Revolution,* in which she gives an account of women in agricultural and factory work, the kind of conditions they lived and worked in, the poverty, lack of food and poor housing. More recently women are increasingly writing their own history — for example *Hidden from History,* Sheila Rowbotham. This book talks about women who were politically active, who fought for birth control and who led strikes.

Though there's a long way to go, it's beginning to be not just a question of 'what did you do in the war, Dad?', but of asking what Mom was doing too!

Other areas reflect the secondary position of women in much the same way. History of art books mention few female painters, and undervalue women's contributions to the arts — decorative arts like embroidery are treated as inferior to painting. The main feeling you get is that only men can be true artists, and this is certainly a view held by many — that most women have failed, in the arts, to be 'great'. Yet there are great women artists who have been virtually ignored, especially in previous centuries.

Books on crafts and technical subjects divide fairly obviously into male and female crafts, even if they don't actually say so. Readers of photography manuals are usually assumed to be men: 'your wife might not be too pleased about your plans for blacking out the bathroom window' is the general tone. Books on flower-arranging usually show women's hands doing the arranging.

In many non-fiction subjects, the fact that women don't write about them enough means we don't get a balanced picture of the world. An example of this is psychology and psychiatry. Until recently, most books in this area were written by men. This means that all kinds of assumptions have been made about how women think and feel that are not necessarily true. It's obvious that there are some things in a woman's life that only women can explain for themselves — men can only talk about how they experience it *as men.* This is particularly true about sexual behavior, pregnancy and childbirth. *The Hite Report,* published in 1976, was the first national survey, by a woman, of women's real feelings toward sex. Many people found the results shocking.

In sociology, the role of woman as housewife and mother has tended to be reinforced rather than questioned. Most of the books in this area are by men. But recently the women's movement has been a very important influence — researching and encouraging others to examine women's attitudes and contributions to society.

With things the way are at the moment, it's much more difficult for girls to imagine doing serious work in painting, writing, history, psychology or whatever — they know their lives will be constantly interrupted with domestic things, some nice, some nasty. Someone once said they doubted whether Mozart had to wash dishes between his composing! If you're a woman, you usually need a lot of money to buy the necessary privacy.

A Room of one's own?

For the sake of making it easier we've divided fiction into 'literature' and 'popular' fiction.

Fiction is an area where women are recognized as having made a huge contribution. Even here, though, in the nineteenth century and into the twentieth, most novels by women had to be written under assumed male names to make sure they got published. The Bronte sisters became Currer, Ellis and Acton Bell: Mary Ann Evans became George Eliot. When it became known that George Eliot was a woman, one critic decided that a novel of hers he'd just given a brilliant review wasn't so brilliant after all.

It wasn't really respectable for women to write novels in the nineteenth century. Jane Austen's friends and relations often had no idea that she was writing. She hid her work every time anyone came into the room, and when caught writing, pretended it was letters or her diary. Virginia Woolf wrote a book about the need for privacy for women, called *A Room of One's Own.* There are plenty of records from diaries of how women tried to get some time to themselves. Mrs. Gaskell used

41

to put on a huge pot of stew immediately after breakfast, leaving it to cook till lunch. Compare this with many male writers' lives — they often had their own studies, were protected from domestic interruptions, didn't have to look after the children or cook meals. (True, they suffered from other things — if they had no private money they had to make a living.) It's amazing that so many great novels were written in the nineteenth century by women, considering the obstacles. Things have obviously improved quite a lot — at least it's now 'respectable' for women to write. But it's still difficult to find privacy, money and time to do it in — though these are luxuries for both sexes.

In literature, women writers are sometimes thought to write best about the minute details of life — the nuances of people's behavior, the ins and outs of human relationships — and not so well about war, government, 'wider issues' of this kind. If this is true at all, which is doubtful, it may reflect the fact that people write best about things they see and experience themselves. Many women writers were limited to the worlds they were familiar with, and they wrote about them movingly and wittily. But what is interesting is that in literature this capacity to write about everyday life is admired by everyone. In *Middlemarch,* one of the most famous of her novels, George Eliot describes life in a provincial town, making one understand people's lives and motives and how complicated these are. Mrs. Gaskell, in *North and South,* gives a picture of what was happening when England began to get industrialized and how it affected people of different background and class.

Some male novelists have shown a more subtle understanding of women than has the world in general. Tolstoy wrote a very moving story about a woman who leaves her husband and goes off with her lover, but is forced to leave her son behind — at a time when people in general weren't very sympathetic, to say the least, to women who did this. Hardy conveys the most complex and painful feelings in some of his women — Tess in *Tess of the D'Urbervilles,* Sue in *Jude the Obscure.* These women's feelings are central to the novels, and are really explored. Perhaps male writers have some freedom from male stereotypes — artists on the whole aren't thought of as 'soft' just because they're sensitive.

But there's a lot of literature written by men that *does* reinforce male values and a male-dominated society — and this is true of 'great' writers as well as of less well-known ones. And, for that matter, of women writers too.

Kate Millett, in a book called *Sexual Politics,* analyzes the work of several modern male writers whose work has been influential and highly praised. She's trying to show that we live in a basically patriarchal society, where men hold power and where masculine values are more important than feminine ones, and that this fact is reflected in literature. She uses the work of D.H. Lawrence, Norman Mailer and Henry Miller to show that in all of them, in different ways, runs the idea that not only *do* men hold power and dominate women, but that they *should* — if they are real men (and women are real women).

Of D.H. Lawrence she says: **'It is unthinkable to Lawrence that males should ever cease to be dominant individualists. So it seems that not only should women submit to them but should do it willingly. To be an independent being in her own right would be unthinkable.'**

Of Henry Miller, she says that he expresses the contempt that masculine culture feels for women, that his women are ridiculed, despised, humiliated and degraded. She feels that if this is how literature reflects male values and its view of women, then 'women perhaps owe something to Miller for letting them know'.

Not everyone agrees with Kate Millett's interpretations — for instance, some people think that Henry Miller is important in that he wrote about sex in a particularly erotic way, which told people something about their sexuality, good or bad. Others think Lawrence's views of women very personal, and that he tried to get at what he thought of as the darker and mysterious forces between the sexes. Of the three, Mailer is perhaps the most universally thought of as a sort of 'defender to the death' of male values.

But whether you agree or disagree, what's important is that Kate Millett wrote the book, and that people are looking at 'great' writers in this way — out of the vacuum of their 'greatness' — to see what their prejudices and conditioning were. It makes us look at writing in a new way.

Unsullied, unspoilt . . .'

While literature is studied at school in textbooks, at colleges and universities in English courses and by many people in their spare time, it's probably true to say that more people read popular fiction than literature. What is popular fiction?

It's basically the cheaply produced books of sex and romance, mysteries, thrillers, spy stories, westerns. They are the kind of books that are neither heavy nor 'serious', that nobody claims are 'good' for you. They are widely available, usually have rather garish covers, and are marketed like any other consumer product. You can find them in libraries, bookshops, railway stations, supermarkets and newsstands.

But why do so many people read these books? — for they are read by literally millions. It's difficult to say exactly why, but perhaps it's something to do with the kind of plots, ideas, language. The plots are almost always based on formulae, and the language and ideas are much less complicated than those of serious novels — so they make fewer demands on the reader. After a hard day's work or on a long train journey, therefore, they are easier to read. The situations described take people out of their daily lives into ones that are usually more exciting and less full of problems.

To do this, not only do the endings have to be happy, but the characters must be uncomplicated, representing extremes — the 'good' woman, the 'brave' man, the 'bitch' — in real life people are usually a bit of everything. This way of writing leads to stereotypes. Reading such books, people escape from their complicated lives into worlds where everything is predictable; the improbable, unreal things are made to seem both desirable and possible.

But of course, these plots are fantasies. And although we all need fantasies at times to have a rest from reality, the difficulty is that often these fantasies confirm ideas we have that are misleading, ideas that have partly been foisted on us by stereotyping in the real world — like the idea that all a woman really needs in life is to find a man to love, and she'll be happy ever after. Readers of these novels lead the usual complicated lives — with their share of happiness and unhappiness, security and insecurity. But it's unthinkable for the heroine of a romance story to marry with the prospect of anything but unending bliss.

If we look at the broad categories of popular fiction, we can see that some are designed to appeal to women, others to men.

Women make up nearly the entire readership of romance stories, whether they're doctor/nurse, secretary/boss, or historical romances. Barbara Cartland is a very famous example of a romance story-writer; Georgette Heyer wrote historical romances. But there are many, many such novels, by known and unknown writers. The covers of the books tend to show an 'ideal' couple, romantically drawn. We'll look at a typical example later.

On the other hand, men make up almost the entire readership of war, adventure and western stories — adult versions of boys' stories. The covers of these books usually show some scene of violence, or a naked woman.

Both men and women read mystery and detective stories, the literary equivalent of the crossword puzzle. The appeal here is slightly different — it's in discovering 'whodunit'. In spy stories we are led into a world of intrigue and courage — readers are often, by implication, invited to identify with the impossible exploits of the hero, his courage, his womanizing (where no one seems ever to get hurt by his amazing pick-them-up-and-drop-them techniques).

To give you an idea of what some of these novels are like, we looked at a few, bought at random from a railway station bookstall. Here's a summary of their plots.

The Khufra Run, by James Graham, and *Stoned Cold Soldier,* by Charles Dennis, were both books likely to be read by men. While very dissimilar in a lot of ways, both featured two men working together and facing an extraordinary challenge. They meet this challenge either because they have more guts and are tougher than the opposition, or because they're smarter and have greater expertise. In contrast, the women are merely incidental figures to the story. In *Stoned Cold Soldier,* the main female character is Cashbox, the Saigon whore, out of reach of the ordinary soldiers and available only to the Ace Reporter. In *The Khufra Run* the female characters fall sharply into two groups. The 'good' woman conveniently turns out to be a nun, the 'bad' woman is an ageing film star, who betrays the heroes to the enemy.

A third woman, a hippy girl, doesn't quite fall into either category. She's always available sexually to the men, but makes no demands on them — sex is just an event; it happens, then it's over. She's a recent stereotype of what a liberated woman is supposed to be — i.e. someone whose sexuality is not complicated by emotion and feeling. It's a convenient stereotype, which in its own way is as much a barrier to understanding women as the more old-fashioned kind. It's interesting that this misleading version of liberation has found its way into these kinds of books — compare these ideas about sexual liberation with the serious writing of someone like Doris Lessing (*The Golden Notebook*).

A Hazard of Heart, by Barbara Cartland (and there are at least 75 other novels of this type by her), and *Tomorrow's Flower,* by Margaret Malcolm, are books much more likely to be read by women. The first is set in some rather vague historical period, the second in the present day. But both are basically about love and marriage: and according to a simple formula, the beautiful girl who remains pure and virginal throughout gets her man despite misunderstandings and treachery by others, etc. The beautiful heroine of *A Hazard of Heart,* Serena, is gambled away by her father. The Marquis of Vulcan (!) has won her in a bet, and she is forced to marry him. At the end of the book he finally comes to realize that he loves her, and explains why he hasn't been very nice to her:

'... because I was cynical, because I had been disillusioned so often by other women, I doubted what I saw with my own eyes. Always I was afraid to obey the instructions of my own heart, always I was trying to catch you out, to find you less pure, less fine than you appeared. I could not believe, you see, that anyone could be so beautiful, so perfect as you — and come to me unsullied, unspoilt.'

There are some typical assumptions here about women —
women are scheming and usually can't be trusted, they're
shallow; in order to be loved as a woman you have to be perfect;
to be perfect you have to be endlessly sacrificing, modest,
sexually untouched. The heroine, on the other hand, makes no
such demands on the man: she doesn't expect him to come to her
"unsullied and unspoilt'. The fact that he's had other women in
his life is neither here nor there — in fact, it might even help to
emphasize *his* stereotype — that he is strong and masterful.
The final kiss convinces her that everything is as it ought to be.

**'She knew, then, his strength, she knew then how strong
and masterful he would always be, and she gloried in it.'**

So we find stereotypes that appear over and over again, in this
type of book. Women are in two groups, the 'good', sexually innocent woman, who gets her reward — her man; the 'bad' woman,
who is often sexually experienced, and makes demands.
Women's true happiness and fulfilment lie only in marriage and
family life. Even if they have a job to begin with, and put up
some misguided struggle to remain independent, they usually
come around to getting their priorities right — marriage comes
first — always.

In *Tomorrow's Flower* for instance, the heroine, Flora, has
neither a career of her own nor any ambitions. The most satisfying work she's ever done turns out to be a little homemaking
for the man she loves and *his* fiancee! She can hardly believe her
luck when she she marries the hero, and becomes the mistress of
a lovely home with a staff of servants at her beck and call.

Most of these stories make it clear that happiness involves a
man *and* money — though most wouldn't be so vulgar as to say
so! In fact they might go to some lengths to imply the opposite
— that love rises above money matters. Yet it's rare to find
happiness and poverty linked in these books.

There are, as we've said, stereotypes for men to live up to as
well. There is the tough, masterful, thin-lipped man who gets
the girl. On the surface he may be difficult to tell from the

other men, except that he's basically honest in some way, including his relationship with the heroine — which might involve him in being honestly dismissive of her! The heroes usually have craggy features and piercing blue eyes; they are the strong silent types. But they are always confident, sure of their decisions. It is these qualities that appeal to the heroines — even though another way of describing them might be bossy, pushy, rigid in their thinking — qualities from which any self-respecting woman would run a mile!

The worst that is said of such men in the novels is that they're arrogant. And that's often a compliment. Homosexuals are not 'real' men, so are never heroes. No hint of softness or effeminancy is tolerated in the heroes. They must never be weak or indecisive. They're allowed to be violent, even brutally so where it's deserved. Even women can be handled roughly by them, so long as they don't overdo it. Men and women are never actually friends. Men are friends only with each other. If men are good, they protect their women: if they're cads, they take advantage of them.

These formulae in popular fiction show men and women in some extreme situations, with characters suitable to their sex, and having little individuality of their own. And the results of their stereotyped behavior are equally stereotyped, as we've tried to show. Yet in real life, these formulae don't guarantee success — it's a much more complex matter. People obviously want to be taken out of their lives at times, to identify with these simple models of heroes and heroines, to know the endings, to escape from reality. The danger is when these formulae are seen as truly attainable and completely desirable. For one thing, they aren't like life, and for another, though most people's lives are more complicated, and often more painful, they are also often more interesting.

Few people would disagree that books are powerful agents in forming ideas and changing attitudes. Some books obviously have much more of an impact than others. Most books, including most popular fiction, are part of the media that influence us all the time, sometimes without our really knowing it, like advertising, films, television and newspapers. These kinds of books tend to lack subtlety and try to provide simple stereotypes which people may try and live up to, because they believe it will make them happy, or that it's expected of them. Other books provide a much more complex view of the world, one that corresponds much more with our actual experiences. They are often very powerful and have great force because of the quality of the writing. There are things we feel that may be difficult to express — good writing can sometimes do it for us.

When you think about history, do you think only about what men did — for example in the Second World War?
Do you have time and space at home to be on your own and write, if you want to? Do you have as much free time as your brothers (if you're a girl) or your sisters (if you're a boy)?
Can you think of any novels written that don't conform to the types we've described?
Do women novelists tend to allow their female characters more scope than male novelists do?
In real life, are passive women more likely to be content than their more adventurous sisters who are less inclined to follow women's traditional roles? Are they likely to be more happy?
Why don't as many men read love stories as women? Why don't as many women read war stories, westerns, etc., as men do?
What sort of books do you like reading? Why?
Have you ever read any of the books of Virginia Woolf, Fay Weldon, Doris Lessing, Edna O'Brien, Colette, Margaret Atwood? What do you think they told you — about women, men, the world?
Have you read any of the books of Norman Mailer or D.H. Lawrence? What did you think of them?

6
THE FILMS YOU SEE

Films are one of the most important areas of twentieth-century art and entertainment, and probably the most difficult and complicated when it comes to discussing the roles played by men and women. For women have been very important and successful on the screen. They have been the greatest stars, loved and identified with by both men and women. They have played many roles and have 'made it' not just because of their looks. For example, stars like Bette Davis and Mae West were successful for their wit and independence, while others like Glenda Jackson and Ellen Burstyn have been admired for their acting ability and powerful interpretation of character.

However, there are various reasons why, in spite of their great importance in film, women have been rather more restricted than men in the roles they play. Men of course have been stereotyped — into tough guys, outlaws and cops, playboys and good guys, but within these parts there is some variety and unpredictability of action. The majority of female stars have been worshipped as heroines and goddesses and this in itself has tended to reinforce the passive role that women are supposed to play in real life. The independent and career-minded women in most films end up proving that they are 'real' women by giving up their independence for Mr. Right when he eventually turns up. When women do have a lot of personality and wit, it tends to be exercised only in a relationship with a man — for example, in the many comedies about marriage. Also, there have been many films made only about men, but until recently, very few made only about women.

Another point is that women's roles in films have tended to become more restricted over the years; they now rarely have the qualities of the great starring roles of the thirties and forties, played by actresses such as Joan Crawford, Barbara Stanwyck, Katherine Hepburn and Bette Davis. Increasingly women in films have fallen into the role of girlfriend, wife, prostitute, mother.

One important reason for women's limited roles on the screen is that as in all other industries, it is very hard for women to get to the top in the cinema world — to be directors and producers. In Britain in 1976 there were only a handful in these jobs, and only three camerawomen. There have been good women directors, like Mai Zetterling and Ida Lupino, and Dorothy Arzner made films in Hollywood, but they have been the exceptions. So, even films with important female characters have usually been directed by men, reflecting a male view of what women are like. The images of women on the screen have been mostly men's images of them.

There is a great variety of forms and standards in films, from art films shown mostly at specialist film clubs to the best in popular films made by well-known and acknowledged directors, to the films that are made only for profit and are found on general release. The kinds of films briefly discussed here are the popular ones that you are most likely to find at your local cinema.

Kung fu fighters

One recent trend in films has been the so-called masculine world of westerns, gangsters, espionage, war and violence. In these films women are wives, girlfriends, secretaries and cleaning women, filling in the background to the men's lives but irrelevant to the central action. Films like *The Sting* and *Butch Cassidy and the Sundance Kid,* featuring a male duo as the stars, have been very successful.

In one sense these films cannot be blamed for ignoring women, or treating them superficially. For the world of excitement, adventure and violence *is* a man's world in which women have very little to do, and the films reflect the world as it is. Have you ever heard of a Jane Bond? a Dirty Harriet? a Godmother? a Midnight Cowgirl? Film-makers are in business; they make the kind of films they think that people will go and see, so that if violence and toughness sells, this is what the films will be about. The current lack of films about women is something of a reflection of women's position in our society.

51

One of the most popular film crazes recently has been for the martial arts and Kung Fu. Men have always been the heroes of fighting and violence, physical strength and combat. Following in the shadow of Bruce Lee, however, there are the female Kung Fu stars, like Angela Mao in *Hap Ki Do,* described as the 'first lady of Kung Fu'. Film directors claimed that this was an example of 'women's lib' in the same way that there are films about female stunt racing drivers. But notice that the women are only copying things that men do. They are being allowed to take a second place in 'male' films as a new gimmick; it's something a bit different to see a woman in a masculine role. This has nothing to do with women being on a par with men, in films made by both sexes and featuring both sexes in a way that is not stereotyped.

Groupie Girls

Another popular theme for films is the world of pop stars, such as *Tommy.* Popular stars are of course men in the films. Women are their admirers; they surround them looking decorative. Which is strange when you think of the great female singers and pop stars around.

Popular 'sexy' films tend to involve little sex, but lots of sexist attitudes. Irresponsible but 'lovable' young men are featured, who 'get through' the vast number of attractive and willing girls who are unable to resist their fatal charms. One such character is Tommy in *Confessions of a Window Cleaner:* he finds it very difficult to keep his mind on the job of window-cleaning because his customers are a delectable lineup of women — all demanding his attentions — a deserted wife, a sexy blonde, a usually naked yoga enthusiast, a stripper, an older lady and a policewoman.

A similar character was Alfie who appeared in a succession of films of the same kind. In his latest he was a long-distance truck driver who collected girls along with his goods. One reviewer commented: 'I think there's a bit of Alfie in every healthy man'.

James Bond is perhaps the best known of the heroes who have a way with girls. Bond's talents as a womanizer is surpassed only by his talent as a secret agent, but we never quite forget which is the most important activity. The women are 'fitted in', as it were, during convenient interludes between his vital missions, and we are left gasping at his incredible energy. To live up to such an image must be a horrifying prospect for any agent who is not superhuman. The women are clearly for one purpose only — one Eastern beauty was aptly named Chew Mee. Another example is Sean Connery's portrayal of a crazy poet in *A Fine Madness*. Despite — or because of — his violence to his wife, she finds him irresistably attractive. So do a variety of other women to whom he also makes love.

The film strip stakes

'A sex symbol is a thing. I hate being a thing.'

Marilyn Monroe

'Any girl can be glamorous. All you have to do is to stand still and look stupid.'

Hedy Lamarr

In 'masculine' films, women are often reduced to becoming little more than sex objects. The greater degree of sexual freedom for women during the last few years has meant that women on the screen can now eagerly leap into bed, whereas previously not only would standards of censorship not allow this, but it was much less realistic to present women as having this kind of freedom.

However, even before the days of nudity on the screen, there were always films in which women were very much exploited for their sexual qualities alone, as happens in life. The Sweater Girls, noted for their curvy figures and tight sweaters, like Jean Harlow and Jane Russell were a huge box office success. Harlow was known to put ice cubes on her bosom to make her nipples more noticeable to the camera. Howard Hughes was Jane Russell's producer, and he sent this memo to her wardrobe department:

The fit of the dress around her breasts is not good and gives the impression, God forbid, that they are padded or artificial. I am not recommending that she go without a brassiere, as I know this is a very necessary piece of equipment for Russell. But I thought, if we could find a half brassiere which will support her breasts upwards and still not be noticeable under her dress, or, alternatively, a very thin brassiere made of very thin material so that the natural contours of her breasts will show through the dress, it will be a great deal more effective . . . it would be extremely valuable if the brassiere, or the dress, incorporated some kind of point at the nipple because I know that does not occur naturally in the case of Jane Russell. Her breasts always appear to be round, or flat, at that point . . .

While Betty Grable had her legs insured for $25,000, more recently the American actress Edy Williams insured her bust for a million dollars. It would be interesting to hear of any male star who had his sexual parts insured because they were essential to his career in films! Some film magazines even keep a record of how many times a star has stripped or been seen in bed on the screen. So things haven't changed much in this kind of film since the days of Jane Russell.

On the good side, you will find some recent films in which women *do* play memorable parts, and in a way that is a development from the days of the 'star' — Julie Christie in *Darling*, Glenda Jackson in *Women in Love*, Jane Fonda in *Klute*, Lily Tomlin in *The Late Show*, Maggie Smith in *The Prime of Miss Jean Brodie*, Chloris Leachman and Sybill Shepherd in *The Last Picture Show*, Faye Dunaway in *Bonnie and Clyde*, Ruth Gordon in *Harold and Maude*, to name just a few.

On the other hand, in many films women are given roles that are a poor reflection of their present status. One example is the film, *Ash Wednesday*, starring Elizabeth Taylor. In this film she plays a 55-year-old American who has lost her former beauty. She has also lost the love of her lawyer husband, although she is still in love with him. In a desperate bid to regain his affection, she decides to undergo total physical transformation by head-to-

toe cosmetic surgery. But she does it without telling him, saying she is going to Italy for a holiday. She arranges for him to join her and plans to surprise him, looking as attractive and desirable as when they first met thirty years earlier.

Her long rejuvenation process is fraught with tension, but the final bandages are removed to reveal a dazzling creature. But will he be pleased? — as she learns with horror, he's on his way firmly resolved to ask for a divorce.

It was considered courageous by some reviewers for one of the screen's most attractive actresses to allow herself to be made up to look so unattractive — but of course, there was the consolation of knowing that, as the rejuvenated woman, she would be allowed to look her glamorous self.

Can you imagine a man playing a role like this? Of course, looks are important to male film stars too, but it's unlikely that they would have to go to these lengths. Can you think of any female film stars who are ugly? For some men are, but their 'ugliness' can be regarded as attractive in itself, or they may just be good actors.

With the development of the women's movement, many women have been thinking about, and working to change, their accepted role in the cinema. Women's film groups and magazines have been set up both in this country and in Europe and the United States. In 1972 the first International Festival of Women's Cinema was held at the National Film Theatre in London. These positive activities by women, and the fact that women's role in society is changing, are signs that we may see new kinds of films and new and more realistic ways of presenting women and men and their relationships in the future. Change may also come as women continue to fight for jobs in the film industry, and as more of them manage to get to the top. Certainly, in the study of sex roles, one of the most interesting things about films is that you will see an enormous contrast between films that are good, and that express real and interesting situations involving men and women, and the poorer ones that stereotype and restrict both sexes into narrow roles. Look out for both kinds and notice very carefully what kinds of roles are played.

Do you know of any women film directors?
Who are your favorite male and female film stars? What sort of
roles do they play? Are the roles very different for each sex?
What was the last film you saw? Were the main characters men
or women? What sort of relationship did the men and women
have with each other?
Have you seen any films in which women are violent?
Can you think of any films mostly about men that are not
violent?

FEMININITY
would mailer still love
Marilyn if she were
alive and well
and fortyeight today?
now that she is safely dead
he says he loved her:
she would have dug that
of course she was a sufferer,
a loser, a shorn lamb,
a moneyspinner
for many hundreds
mailer included
and of course the culture
killed her by its lethal dose
of bright lights/intrusion/stereotyping
and of course her immortality
lies in the film cans
that hold her reeling

she was femininity writ grand
a larger than life mutilation
with whom my mother identified;
it takes one victim
to smell another

Astra

Who are Mailer and Marilyn? What do you know about them?

PART TWO:

THE MEDIA

THE FINISHED PRODUCT

Mr Media

Mrs Media

Tall, dark, handsome
working model
Guaranteed
indefinitely
improves with age
Power-driven

Where would you be
without him?
An essential item

A life-long
investment

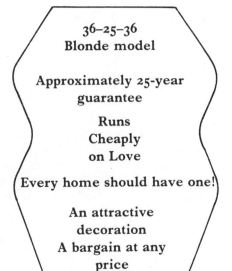

36–25–36
Blonde model

Approximately 25-year
guarantee

Runs
Cheaply
on Love

Every home should have one!

An attractive
decoration
A bargain at any
price

PART TWO:

1
THE MEDIA THEY FEED YOU

What we see has become more important than what we hear. The mass media are important because they put across a picture of the world that we are exposed to all the time. Often we're not really aware of what is being put across, but in fact the messages are slowly filtering through to us and affecting our ideas about ourselves and other people.

One of the most powerful agents of the mass media in forming our ideas of the world is the advertisement. This is the one thing in our society that you can never completely get away from. It's in the street, on the screen, in print and on the air. It's set to music, it's large and vivid. We're so used to seeing ads that we hardly notice their total impact on us.

Put together, they present what appears to be the only ideal and desirable way of living, a life-style that everyone should aim for. They define what is in style and what is good taste. They don't do this crudely, but by suggestion. The unspoken message is that this is how things *are,* or at least how they *should* be, not that they are ideas and possibilities. By leaving out everything that does not fit in with this pattern, the message is 'this is how everybody is — so why aren't you?' The style and taste put across may not be yours, but it's you who will be made to feel inferior.

The world of the ads is that of the well-off middle class as seen through the eyes of the admen. This small group defines 'the good life' for the rest of us. Although we know that the world in the ads isn't the world we live in, the men and women in them represent what 'ideal' people are like. We are encouraged to try to be like them.

For the 'good life' you need money. It is mostly women who decide how money is spent on consumer goods. So most advertisements are aimed at women. Women are bombarded with images of themselves with which they can identify. They think:

'I want to be like her'. Even though we're talking about advertising here, the same type of women appear constantly in all the media. They're not real, but ideal types, to which ordinary women aspire.

Are you the right type?

Basically there are five main types of image for women, three of which appear in nearly all the advertisements and two of which appear less frequently:
(1) the Carefree Girl
(2) the Career Woman
(3) the Hostess
(4) the Wife and Mother
(5) the Model

The Carefree Girl

Notice that we say carefree *girl* and not woman. This is deliberate. The carefree girl in the ads is the one who is having a good time while she's still young. She is not carefree for any particular reason — only because she has not settled down yet. She's free, yes, but not free to do anything in particular apart from enjoy herself, which means to buy things.

She is the one you probably identify with if you are a young and unmarried girl. She's the vehicle for selling the fun things in life, at the time of your life when you can spend on yourself, indulge in the latest or most bizarre fashion craze. She will not be able to do this later in life, when she has a husband and family to put first.

Bite into a Golden Crunchie
and give a little smile...

The Career Woman

A type that occurs less often is the career woman, but notice: the careers themselves are usually 'women's work' as described in Book 1 of this series. That is, women shown in these ads are usually secretaries or nurses and the advertisements themselves are noticeably duller and less appealing to the eye than those in which we see glamorous models selling hair sprays or cars.

Working wives rarely appear in ads. The impression you get is that most women don't have to work for a living — they're kept by their fathers or husbands or boyfriends. If you believed these ads you'd never realize that women are 40% of the work force!

Of the two main types, we shall look at next, you will see that, although they differ slightly from each other, they still show women as having only one fixed goal in life. There are two paths to this goal, but the goal is always the same — the home and family.

One way of achieving this goal is by being noticeably beautiful, fashionable and sophisticated. This means also having a home with the latest gadgets. The other way is by being traditionally feminine and natural, having children and creating a pleasant cozy home. The first is on show, a public life-style, while the second is more private and centered around the family. Both paths take it for granted that the only place for a woman is the home. Because we see women in these roles all the time, we are led to think that this is the only thing a woman can do that will be approved by society.

So for housewives and mothers, the media not only show approval of what they are doing, but reassure them that it is the 'right' thing.

The Hostess

This is the lady of leisure, usually seen entertaining or giving expensive dinner parties. Her home is perfectly tidy, tastefully decorated, very modern. It's never unfashionable, dull or messy.

At home at the most beautiful dinners in America.

This is because her home is a reflection of her, and she is very much concerned with the objects around her: her hostess cart, the latest stove, a deep freezer, stylish furniture. As there is nothing outside the home for her this is her identify, so it must be as perfect as she can make it. She has produced this perfect little world but she can never escape from it. There is never any suggestion that it could sometimes be a depressing or an un-satisfying way of life.

The Wife and Mother

The wife and mother is also usually seen in the home, or at least in the local neighborhood. The home for her, as for the hostess, is very important. Not because it's fashionable, but because that is where her duties lie. Her house tends to be ordinary and looks lived in by her family. She's never as glamorous as the other three types — often she will be older, plainer and more practical. She's never seen in exotic or sophisticated clothes — but on the other hand she doesn't wear working clothes, either — which suggests that what she is doing as wife and mother is not actually work. She doesn't spend her time on herself, but on looking after her husband and family. Her image is a busy one; she has a lot to do, all of which is worthwhile and satisfying. Most of the time she is calm and content, but now and then the strains show through and she has a headache, or is unable to cope. But a Brand X tablet soon cures that, leaving her happy and smiling. Then she can cheerfully face the load of ironing lying in the background.

The Model

She bears the least resemblance to real life. For the most part she advertises clothes and makeup. She's cool, distant and untouchable. The background will always be an exotic, unusual, perhaps slightly fantastic one. She'll never be seen taking out the garbage or lugging groceries. As a beautiful object she is on show all the time and will never let herself down.

We haven't said very much about men. Men are just as stereotyped as women. They roughly fall into the following types:
(1) Husband and father
(2) Boyfriend/friend
(3) Model
(4) Worker
(5) He-man/hero

Look at some advertisements; what qualities do the people in
them have? Try comparing them with the types of women we've
discussed. Where and how do they differ?

From thinking about these types, what qualities would you say
the Ideal Man and the Ideal Woman are supposed to have?
Have any ads that you have seen been anything like the people
you know or the way you live?

2
THE WAY YOU LOOK

Makeup — what they say

A mixed group of teenagers had this to say when asked why girls wear makeup:

I'm a fourteen-year-old, but when I'm dressed up and wearing makeup I could get in to see any X film that I wanted to. The thing is nowadays that people tend to judge us by the way our face looks.

Teenagers wear it because they think it is part of becoming a woman. Older women, like my Mom, wear it because they feel they are expected to look their best, to compete with younger women.

Makeup is mainly used by girls to bring out their best features, to attract boys. An older person will use it to hide their age. It's also used to hide spots, scars or cuts, so that the complexion will look better.

I wear it to look different, out of the ordinary. . .

Every morning when I get up I look in the mirror. I seem so ugly to myself, but as I put on pan stick, powder, rouge, lipstick and mascara I seem to have another kind of face — more mature and attractive.

When asked why boys did not wear makeup to the same extent as girls, the replies were:

I don't think boys will ever wear makeup because makeup makes the skin look softer and boys don't really want this. They want to look stronger and more rugged.

Men are the more sensible of the species so they don't wear it . . .

Boys don't wear it because they really don't care what they look like. A few might want to wear it but they wouldn't dare. If they did they would be called some awful names . . .

Girls have to wear it to make boys notice them; if they're plain they have to stand out in a crowd. Boys don't need make-up to get themselves noticed.

Beauty is all that is demanded

To be beautiful is enough! If a woman can do that well who shall demand more from her? You don't want a rose to sing.

Thackeray

Her face is fortune.

What would you think if you saw a man take out a mirror in public and start doing his hair and examining his nose? Would you be likely to think it strange behavior? No one thinks it unusual when a woman takes out her compact and powders her nose in a restaurant, or constantly rushes to the 'ladies room' to check that her appearance is still perfect. What is seen as normal vanity in a woman would be ridiculous in a man.

From the TV serial *Softly, Softly:*

Detective — 'How would you like that then — to have your face slashed?'
Male suspect — 'Oh, I don't know — women like that sort of thing.'

But do they? What do you think?

For a man to have his face scarred doesn't ruin his life, nor does it make him feel that he is unlovable and ugly. It could even make him more masculine and thus more attractive to the opposite sex. But the prospects for a woman who has her face scarred permanently are entirely different. In fact, this is even recognized in our courts of law. A woman who is scarred as a result of, say, a car accident, will be very likely to get high damages awarded her. The reasoning is simple: she is less attractive — 'damaged' — and her chances of finding a husband are therefore decreased. So she is compensated for that.

Good looks in a man are a bonus, not a necessity. But people are less tolerant of ugliness in women. If they are ugly they are expected to do something about it. This is not to say that men do not care whether they are good looking or not, because they do. They suffer if they have acne, or if they are going bald, but basically it's accepted that they don't need to tamper with themselves. They can alter their hair or dress a bit more fashionably, but they are not expected actually to *disguise* what they are really like.

In fact, 'masculinity' to a large extent means not caring very much about one's looks and not expecting compliments and flattery.

Men, by and large, are not tempted to make beautiful objects of themselves. Neat, clean and healthy, yes, but beautiful object — never.

Women, from their earliest years, are taught that there is something more required of them. They are taught the importance of looking good. Society expects women from childhood on to take a greater interest in their appearance than men. They are conditioned to show greater concern with their faces and bodies and to please men by their looks. This is put very well in this letter to a magazine:

Flicking through some old copies of your magazine, I came across a letter from Michael Smith, the misjudged male who says that we girls never have to fish out money when going on a date.

70

This just isn't true! When a girl is asked out, of course she wants to look her best, to impress the boy. So she probably spends the money she's saved to buy a new LP on new clothes! She wants her hair in good condition so she spends money at the hairdresser's or on a new shampoo. Then she'll probably buy a new eye shadow or a new nail polish, plus a pair of panty hose.

When you add all that up it comes to quite a bit. Mere males like Michael don't have to go through all that — they only have to pay a couple of bus fares and about $3.00 each to get into a disco or the pictures.

So they don't do too badly, do they?

— a Mere Female

Even when women are involved in something serious, such as political protest, the only thing that is assumed to be of ay importance by the media is their looks. So you will often find headlines such as:

'Pretty face of protest in a nurses' rally'

The emphasis placed on looking good is brought out in the experience of one woman who decided to retrain for a new job, and took a shorthand typing course at college:

THE LESSER SPOTTED SECRETARY BIRD

We had lectures on 'business organization' — being told how important it is to keep good time at work, and how to discipline others who don't. We were instructed in how to make coffee for the boss, and how to arrange his flowers. And worst of all, we had two compulsory days of makeup, fashion and hairdressing . . .

. . . I refused to have makeup put on or to put any on myself. Having explained to the 'instructor' that this was my personal

decision and that I was quite willing to stay in the salon for the compulsory two and a half hours, I was amazed at the attack which was immediately launched at me. 'Oh, I've met people like you,' snarled the instructor. 'You must have had some dreadful experience to make you feel this way about makeup.'.
— A woman's magazine, November 1974

Have you ever heard of an apprenticeship or training course for men containing lessons on good grooming or 'making the most of yourself'?

People have said that my products are too expensive, but they're the people who do not understand that real security is only achieved by feeling beautiful.

Estee Lauder

Real security for women, that is. For men, that would come from other things. Girls are led to believe that being beautiful and making the most of their 'femininity' will lead to certain rewards:
(1) the satisfaction of just being beautiful: nothing else will be expected of you — just that you stay that way as long as possible;
(2) love and romance: by being beautiful a girl stands a far, far greater chance of a boy noticing and falling for her.

Research carried out at the University of Rochester showed that pretty girls are status symbols. Men are attracted to pretty girls because they recognize their status value. Men themselves considered they would be thought more of with a pretty, rather than a plain girl.

How important is it for your girlfriend to look good? Do you expect her to take more trouble than you?
If you are a girl, do you think you've got a better chance in life if you're good-looking?

Love yourself — narcissism

'Next to myself I like Vedonis.'

In the ancient myth, Narcissus was a young man who fell in love with his own image.

That is what women are encouraged to do, to admire themselves and be deeply involved in their looks.

Women are supposed to get a great deal of satisfaction from just being beautiful. This comes across most strikingly in ads for makeup, beauty preparations, hair products and underwear. In these ads the woman is shown as:

(1) completely wrapped up in herself, often in a sort of trance, with a soft expression on her face;

(2) usually having her hair long rather than short. Very often it is blonde to suggest innocence and purity. Often she wears few clothes or even none at all;

(3) caressing and admiring her own body and involved only in the beauty and sensuality of it.

Look at the ads for men's underwear — are the men presented in this way? Are they ever shown admiring their own bodies? What is the difference between liking yourself as a person and being wrapped up in your own looks?

The transformation scene

How often have you heard:
Why doesn't she do something with herself?
She'd look so much better if only she . . .
She doesn't make the most of herself.
If only she lost 20 pounds, got her hair styled. . .
She doesn't bother with makeup. . .
Why don't you have a new hairdo/buy a new dress? Something to cheer yourself up.

73

All these expressions suggest that by doing something to yourself (mainly to your hair, face and figure, and by using various aids) you will somehow be:
   happier with yourself;
   happier with life;
   more acceptable as a person.

'Yourself' is only what you look like — nothing more. It is only that which other people can see and judge. And what is seen is your face, hair and figure, and you have to make them as attractive as possible . . . if you are a female, that is. Any ordinary male would laugh uproariously if you asked him to undergo the sort of 'beauty routine' his girlfriend undertakes for him. Few men can even be persuaded to try on makeup 'just for a laugh'. They protest that they will be stared at in the street if they wear it. But isn't that precisely one of the reasons why women wear it?

Magazines often give women advice on how to get 'the most out of life'. But often this only means improving their appearance. Even the most ordinary and unglamorous of moms can have something done to her to make her look somewhat better. Deep in the heart of even the plainest girl is the desire to be transformed. This wonderful improvement is available with a little help and effort — and, of course, money.

One very common way of putting this across comes in the 'transformation' article in magazines, where 'before' and 'after' photographs of readers are compared. The women are photographed as they normally are — the implication being that this was not good enough. Then they are photographed 'after' the beauty and fashion makers have arranged for them to be 'improved' one way or another.

She came to us wearing trousers, a bright shirt and clumpy shoes, with long hair in a loose straight unflattering style. THE ANSWER was to go in for the new-length look which particularly suited her height. We dressed her in this cord pinafore and multi-colored shirt, and set her hair in soft pretty curls.

From a women's magazine

74

But the ultimate in 'transformation' is making yourself into someone actually glamorous, possibly like a film star or model.

LOVELIGHT THE WAY TO FAME
Faces are made famous by . . . LOVELIGHT.
See Frances arrive at the premiere:
The crowd surges around,
Her glamor fills the night with admiring faces.
She's the star,
And she shines because of . . .
LOVELIGHT . . . let it shine on you!

To go one stage further, the cosmetic ads are saying in fact that by using their makeup your face can almost become a work of art:

> By using your face as a canvas, getting to know its planes and rises, you could paint on another shape, giving yourself hollow cheeks and a slimmer nose. We show you how — the better way.
> — From a women's magazine

Have you ever thought that your life would be much better if only you could change the way you looked?
What do boys do to be noticed and attract the attention of the opposite sex?

It's hard work looking natural

Makeup can be worn for a dramatic effect, but in recent years it is mostly worn with another effect in mind — to look natural, as innocent as possible. You can wear a great deal of it, have eyelashes and nails that are false, have a tan that is fake, wear a wig — as long as it looks 'natural', all is well.

In keeping with this trend, cosmetic manufacturers have used the message again and again that their products are 'natural' or

75

made from 'natural ingredients' or, when applied, will give you a 'natural look' — forgetting in all this wearing any makeup at all is a very unnatural thing to do.

Makeup that is waterproof, cryproof and even 'love-proof' is heavily advertised, so that if a woman even swims, cries or makes love her mascara won't run, and her face will still look 'natural'.

So by buying expensive cosmetics you can disguise an unhealthy look. To get a glow on your face you are told to buy rouge and cheek gloss — not to take strenuous walks. If you *really* want to look natural you don't need makeup — only an adequate diet and exercise, something that cannot be sold over the counter. There are very few 'cosmetics' that you actually need to buy: such as lip-salve if your lips crack.

Notice how all these advertisements stress the 'natural side of makeup' (our italics):

NATURE'S CHILD
Our Special Health cosmetics are *made with nature's ingredients:* honey, wheatgerm oil, beeswax, almond oil, extracts of camomile, coltsfoot, sage, all of nature's wonders, to make you
. . . NATURE'S CHILD.

FANTASTIC FACE GLOSSERS
Clear transparent face color. To get the sunshine in your face. Glow with health all year round with our see-thru, clearly fantastic, natural shades, Pure Gold, Pure Tan, Pure Copper, Pure Honey . . .
FROM FANTASTIC . . . NATURALLY!

You may well say there's nothing wrong with wearing makeup — in fact, it's nice to. Then why don't men?
If you are a girl, have you ever refused to go as far as the corner shop without your makeup on?
If you are a boy, have you ever tried going to the corner shop *with* makeup on?

'Forever 21, I'd be afraid to stop'

In the never-ending search to be young and beautiful, women are expected to pay a great deal of attention to their skin.

There is a whole lot more to it than mere soap and water — a whole industry of enormous complexity, geared to keeping one's skin looking younger than it really is.

It is assumed from the beginning that in her efforts to attract a partner of the opposite sex, a girl's skin is of utmost importance. It can make or break a relationship, or the possibility of one. So to make her skin as perfect, flawless and touchable as possible a girl has to spend a great deal of time, effort and money. A girl will be constantly reminded that:

Your skin is your appeal
> — Advertisement for face pack

'The *Gentle* way to deep, deep cleanse' — in case you thought a good wash was enough, it obviously isn't!

If you don't have a perfect skin, then you could be forgiven for thinking that you are totally repulsive and offensive, and for thinking that no self-respecting male could bring himself to come anywhere near you, much less kiss you.

To judge from the ads, the worst fate that could befall a woman is for her skin to lose its 'youthful dewy tinge' and to start to age — and even worse, for wrinkles to appear. Notice that on men wrinkles and lines on the face are a sign of 'maturity' and an attractive feature.

Do people guess your age too easily?
> — Advertisement for a skin oil

A great many products for skin stress the importance of keeping the skin 'moisturized'. Should you fail to do this, then you have only yourself to blame if your skin shrivels and withers till it resembles a dry prune.

So the twin threats of 'dryness' and 'lines' become real enemies that must be fought off at all costs. Women will spend amazing sums of money on skin creams and lotions that promise that they will get rid of lines and wrinkles. And the real 'con' is that many of these products don't work any better than the cheapest and most basic ones.

In the search for the ever-youthful skin, women are encouraged to try everything from processed clay, limes, avocados, eggs, cucumbers, to cactus and vitamin extracts — all of which, they are assured, will leave their skin 'improved'.

Even the slightest difference in a skin care product is hailed as a scientific or even a miraculous breakthrough. It is on a par with more important social or medical discoveries.

How many jars and bottles of face creams, etc., have you got? Do they work? Do you think they are worth spending money on?

'A good investment'

The way women have been persuaded to take their looks very seriously can be seen in the money they spend.

Women spend $60 million a year on cosmetics.
Men spend $25 million. But this is on:
40% after shave
20% colognes
30% hairdressing/conditioners
10% shaving products.

Nova

A quick glance through the 1977 price list of a well-known beauty salon reveals the lengths women will go to, and the amount they will spend, in search of beauty:

Main Chance Day (includes steam bath, massage, facial, makeup and light lunch) $75.00
Miracle Morning $55.00

Application of individual eyelashes — top and
    bottom $25.00
Paraffin bath with 30 minute massage $15.00
Oil manicure $6.00

                        Elizabeth Arden Beauty Salon

The price list is actually five pages long and covers every single
area of the body.

As well as beauty salons, there are beauty advisers who call
around to the house. Some makeup firms realized how profit-
able it would be if they could reach the household woman who
had neither the time nor the energy to search around the shops.
These are the very women who welcome an outside visitor, even
though she's selling something. It's a welcome break in the day.
One advertisement offers:

**'Your very own beauty adviser in the peace and quiet of
your own home. Sounds like VIP treatment — and that's
just what it is.'**

Women are encouraged to change and improve their looks not
only by the use of makeup and by dieting but also in more
drastic ways. Plastic, or cosmetic, surgery is not covered by most
insurance plans except in very special cases. To have it done
privately is very expensive, but the investment is considered
worth it if you have a new nose or a younger-looking face at the
end of the costly and painful procedure:

minor: getting rid of bags under the eyes $150 - $300
medium: nose reshaping, breast enlargement $700 and up
major: full facelift, breast reduction $1,000 and up

If you're male, try putting on a full face makeup. Does it improve
your looks? How do you feel about wearing it? How do other
people react to you?

New!
Makeup that helps skin over 25 look younger.

Introducing Cover Girl®
'MoistureWear'

When you're under 25, a smooth, natural look may be all you want from makeup. But over 25, your makeup should do more. Smooth out tiny, dry skin lines. Add a warmer depth of color to put a few more roses in your cheeks. That's why Cover Girl created 'MoistureWear'™Makeup. Makeup with a balanced blend of special moisturizers, and fresh, fresh color to instantly improve the look of skin over 25. And help you look better than you have in years. 'MoistureWear' is pre-moisturized. So dewy you need no moisturizer underneath. Wear it and you can look the way you want to look —younger, fresher, prettier!

Also available: Nighttime Moisturizer, Moisturizing Under Eye Cover Stick, Moisturizing Wrinkle Stick.

If you don't normally wear makeup — what is the reason? Do people ask you why you don't? Would you ever wear it for a 'special occasion'?

If you do wear it — why? How do you think it affects your looks? How much money do you spend on makeup — and on your appearance in general? Do you wear it to make yourself older or younger?

Have you ever thought seriously about changing the shape of your nose or ears, or your body in general? Why would you want to do this?

Would you enjoy spending six hours having a beauty treatment?

Dedicated follower of fashion

Girls often say that one good thing about being female is being able to dress how they like and to wear nice clothes. It is seen as one advantage they have over boys. But is it really? What it means is that, in the effort to be noticed, to stand out from the others, you have to follow the latest fashion craze. It could be hot pants or granny dresses, midis, mini-skirts or the 1940s look. But it must be the look of the moment, with all the right accessories to go with it. With dedication you achieve the look — but six months later you shudder to think what made you actually wear *that*.

Glamor girl in an exciting outfit — sweet girl in a pretty little smock — thoughtful girl in a long, flowing dress — they're all you.

Dress like a little old lady and bring back a little grace to your life.

This constant change of look is a gold mine for the fashion industry. Girls cannot expect their clothes to last, because they are both badly made and likely to become old-fashioned very quickly. They can also be an indulgence, something to buy to cheer yourself up with, like an extravagant box of chocolates:

81

TREAT YOURSELF

Many girls think that spending money on underwear and nighties is a waste. They'd rather spend their hard-earned cash on things that are seen (more often) by the public at large. So it really is a luxurious treat when you splurge on a little nothing nightie or bra and pants. Try treating yourself to these 'nothings' *to help you over the miserable months.* Nightie $25 and bra and panties $8.50.

The clothes women wear tend to restrict their movement more than men's clothes do. An example of this can be seen in the shoes they wear: from deforming three-inch pointed stilettoes to huge stacked platforms.

There are also clothes that are designed to be 'sexy and seductive', and it is wives and girlfriends who wear them. 'Sexy and seductive' clothes include garter belts, transparent purple or black negligees, incredibly tight-fitting and slinky dresses, cutaway bras.

Do you think girls spend more on clothes than boys? Are fashionable clothes more important for a girl than for a boy? Do you like buying clothes? If so, why?

Be some body — 'my girdle is killing me'

Not only is a woman's face judged, but so is her body, which must be not only beautiful but also desirable. Men, it seems, are attracted to a woman more because of her body than her face. So a great deal of persuasive propaganda is aimed at women in the form of slimming aids. Sometimes the message is put in its crudest form:

FAT AND LONELY — SLIM AND DESIRABLE

As no one wants to be lonely and miserable, the message hits home, and so does the belief that slimness will somehow solve all her problems:

I LOST 38lbs IN 6 SHORT WEEKS
I was a sad, fat figure . . . then EASYSLIM transformed not
only my figure, but my whole life. I am now slim, attractive,
happy and contented.

Kate Turner

While nobody wants to be fat or overweight — in fact, it can
be dangerous and unhealthy — women who are not actually
overweight at all are told they must be *thin*.

There is a whole range of products designed to suppress your
appetite, slimming foods that are cardboard imitations of real
foods at almost twice the price and include such delicacies as
low-cal veal parmigiani, and a 'whole meal in a cookie; To diet
and to lose weight is presented as an achievement, a success
story:

'5' MINUTE BODY SHAPER
We care about the shape you're in — DON'T YOU?

The kind of pressure on a woman to be slim does not show
concern with her feelings, but with what other people will think
of her. The desire to become slim, and therefore to be a success,
can lead to obsession. There is a condition called *anorexia
nervosa* which affects mainly adolescent girls. They starve
themselves over a long period of time to a state where they
become seriously ill. It's unusual to hear of a boy suffering from
this illness.

In the effort to make her body approximate a distant ideal, a
lot of a girl's anxiety centers around her breasts. Usually they
are either too big or too small, depending on what is currently
the popular look. The amount of exposure breasts get make it
obvious that most of a girl's attractiveness depends on them
being the 'right size'.

To get the 'right size' the only methods that are of any use are
quite drastic — only surgery can make breasts smaller, and to
make them larger there are such things as silicone injections.
There are other methods widely advertised, such as bust
developers:

83

"Thanks to Prolamine, I don't need a girdle anymore."

Mrs. Nancy Hogan, Mentor, O.

"Has Prolamine helped me? Emphatically, yes. 24 years ago my husband said he'd divorce me if I ever got fat. Well, I've never become fat, but like most women, somehow 10 to 15 excess pounds gradually sneaked up on me. A sad and disgusting sight is a body that looks like a stuffed sausage. I called a halt to my sideways growth with Prolamine Time Capsules and Diet Plan. And I didn't need a girdle anymore. Now I'm just about at my ideal weight and I intend to continue using the Prolamine Reducing Plan."

"I weighed 227 pounds. With the help of The Prolamine Reducing Plan, I now work as a model."

Elizabeth Grims, Gibsonia, Pa.

"78 pounds ago, people used to tell me what a pretty face I have. But I'm sure they must have thought, 'It's a shame she's so fat.' I am 5'10" and used to weigh 227 pounds. With the help of Prolamine, I lost all that grotesque fat. Now I am working as a model. But best of all, I feel healthy and happier now. Of course, there is a drawback. I have to cope with a jealous husband, but I like that! Prolamine helped me lose weight and now it helps me maintain my figure."

"I went from 205 lbs. to 140. The Prolamine Reducing Plan really changed my life, including my love life!"

Linda Jackson, Houston, Tex.

"Once I found Prolamine, I stopped taking the other diet products. I tried Ayds, but could not get used to drinking hot beverages everytime I took one. Figure-Aid didn't do anything for me either. At first, I didn't think Prolamine would work. Then, my mother and sister watched in amazement as I slowly withered down. My goal was 150 lbs. I now weigh 140. They used to call me, 'Big Momma.' Now they call me 'Slim.' Thanks to Prolamine Time Capsules and Diet Plan, my life has really changed, especially my love life. I should have written to you before this, but I've been enjoying my new size so much that I simply forgot."

The Prolamine Plan works for thousands to help take weight off.

Thousands of users from all across the country have written about their successful weight losses on the exciting Prolamine Reducing Plan. Prolamine Time Capsules work continuously to help you control your appetite, not just at mealtime, but between meals, too. Now lose pound after pound, inch after inch of ugly, unhealthy fat as you follow this outstanding, successful diet plan. Join the thousands of satisfied, successful Prolamine weight-losers . . . you **can** lose weight, you **can** slim down to your slimmest, most attractive size figure. Start the Prolamine Time Capsule Diet Plan today. See how soon you are wearing smaller sizes, smarter fashions.

Available At All Leading Drug Counters. © 1977 Thompson Medical Co., Inc.

> Don't feel left out of the latest fashion ideas because your bustline isn't up to it. Makeabust helps to replace that sag look with high firm breasts.

But as consumer reports have shown, very few of these aids actually work.

The effort to alter your figure doesn't stop with dieting — there are also foundation garments. Victorian ladies were famous for the lengths they would go to in order to have a tiny fashionable waist of around sixteen inches. Women now might not go to quite the extremes their grandmothers went to, but they are still persuaded to 'control' and corset their figures, which, if the ads are to be believed, threaten to spread so that the slightest roll of fat becomes an ugly threat.

How often have you heard a woman describe her *vital* statistics, her bust, waist, and hip measurements?

An attractive woman? Well, she's 36-25-36.

Chances are you have never heard a man described like this.

Have you ever seen a man in a diet advertisement?
If you are a boy, have you ever felt you must be slim?

Crowning glory

Ever noticed just how many 'top' hairdressers and stylists are men? Vidal Sassoon, Michaeljon . . .

Hair has always been a symbol of sexuality. A hairy face, chest, legs, armpits and arms are perfectly acceptable — but only if it's on a man. With it, he will be regarded as attractively masculine. The only place where men are not expected to have more hair than women is on their heads. But when it became fashionable for men to grow their hair, they proved that their locks were the equal of their girlfriends!

On a woman, however, any hair anywhere on her body is automatically seen as superfluous and disgusting, to be got rid of as soon and as quickly as possible. Hair on legs, under the arms or on her face is a threat to 'femininity' and there are a whole host of treatments that can be used to remove it. They range from painless depilatory creams, 'ladies' razor' for shaving, through to waxing and electrolysis treatments. In some cases women have even been known to shave off their pubic hair, in the belief that they are thus more feminine. The tradition in oil painting has often shown the nude female as a totally hairless creature, without even pubic hair.

Beauty begins with clear, smooth hair-free skin....DERMA TWEEZ away unwanted hair forever.

In the effort to stay as smooth and hairless as possible, one international beauty was reported as regularly plucking out every individual hair on her legs with tweezers! But there are simpler ways:

For weeks and weeks of silky smooth shaving, pick a Daisy. After all, Daisy is recommended by millions of pretty, smooth legs!

But hair on the head is an entirely different matter. Women are encouraged to lavish an enormous amount of loving care and attention on their hair — to the extent of wearng wigs, or as the ads say, having a 'wardrobe of them to go with your every change of mood'. One wig consultant in a department store had this to say about them:

They aren't considered unusual anymore because they're becoming essential. They're even more essential if you have got a job in the public eye, to make sure you look smart and well-groomed all the time. Sales are absolutely booming.

It's only when they are going bald that men will actually consider the possibility of wearing a toupee.

But above all else, hair is seen as something wild which has to be tamed, made manageable, kept under control. At the slightest provocation it will disintegrate into a wild mess.

If you are a woman, just keeping your hair clean is no simple matter. First of all you have to choose from a bewildering variety of shampoos, all of which promise to do far more for your hair than merely get rid of the dirt.

After shampooing comes the ritual of conditioning, treating split ends, drying your hair, straightening it if it is curly or curling it if it is straight.

So why take all this trouble? The reason is simple: men notice and desire women who have beautiful hair. On this point the ads are very explicit:

Men are turned on by full-bodied healthy hair, so give yourself a head start, use Thickset.

Notice just how many blondes you see in the ads and just how few you see in real life. Statistically blondes are a minority in the population. Having long fair hair is a symbol of what is desirable in a woman. By going blonde you are assured of all the best things in life.

If you don't want to go blonde then there are other changes:

I'm a naturalist! That's why Nice 'n Easy is a natural for me.

If Clairol can't put color in your life, nobody can.

Hair products are perhaps one of the worst examples of the commercial exploitation of women. For example, research has shown that most shampoos do nothing more than wash the hair; they do not add the special proteins, vitamins and tonics that they claim to. Not only can hair preparations be of doubtful benefit — they can even be harmful. American research has suggested that there could be a connection between the use of hair dyes and lung cancer.

How often have you heard women referred to by their hair color — as gorgeous blondes, cuddly brunettes or sexy red heads? But have you ever heard men referred to in the same way?

Smells

Want him to be more of a man? Try being more of a woman.

Perfume ad

If you are a woman, then you are not expected to smell at all but to be completely odorless and deodorized. All natural smells are removed to be replaced with perfumes — because the expectation is that women ought to smell nice, and that natural smells are offensive. The smells of beer, sweat or tobacco on men are quite acceptable because they are 'masculine' smells.

Women wear men's perfumes sometimes, but never the other way around. Men wouldn't be caught dead wearing a woman's perfume — they'd be called fairies. Very few men like to wear cologne — which is more or less what after-shave lotion is — they would rather 'After shave' was written on the bottle. They don't want to be thought effeminate.

Every single woman wears makeup and perfume for men. There is no other reason. No matter what price it is women are still going to buy it.

Perfume consultant

What's the first thing a girl should put on after her shower? Oder-Less.

Your answer might well be, her clothes — but no. It turns out that she should be putting on, or spraying on, her vaginal deodorant. This has been the marketing success story of recent years. Millions of people have already been persuaded to deodorize their armpits, mouths and feet in order to become socially acceptable. So the marketing men turned their attention to another sensitive area. This time it was a specifically female fear that was exploited. Not only were women persuaded that their sexual parts had a smell, but that it was actually repellent and could prove to be a grave social problem. There was an attempt to launch a male equivalent called 'Lui', but it never caught on — men, it seems, refuse to believe in the need for an 'intimate' deodorant.

Women were sold on the idea that 'vaginal odor' was as much a problem as any other deodorizing problem. To have any confidence at all in themselves the ads assured us that 'bathing and showering are just not enough' and that to 'feel fresh, cool and confident all day long you need something more'. That something is an aerosol spray in various pretty perfumes such as Fleur, Herbe and Sophistique, to mask any claim to a natural smell you might have.

The ads get at the confidence of women in themselves. It seems confidence can only really be attained for the price of a deodorant. This fact is actually spelt out in the advertisements:

Just a 2-second spray gives you the confidence of knowing you'll stay fresh for hours.

They are made to appear necessary, 'an essential part of your makeup'. The reverse is true. Soap and water are enough. If it turns out they aren't, then there is likely to be something medically wrong, so it would be a good idea to see a doctor. Merely disguising any truly offensive smell does not help.

The ads claim that these intimate deodorants are 'medically approved' and 'recommended by leading chemists', but they make no mention that they have been known to cause allergies, severe irritation and soreness:

At the peak of the vaginal deodorant boom, 1 in 3 girls between the ages of 16 and 24 were buying them. The younger the woman, the easier she is to persuade.

89

Sales have now dropped — perhaps women aren't so easy to persuade after all!

Join the freedom lovers

When you look at ads notice just how many of them have used the slogans of Women's Liberation in order to sell their products. The rights and freedoms women are struggling to get have been trivialized and twisted. What is offered by advertisers is the freedom to move easily in your panty girdle. So women's bodies are used to adorn subway stations while they claim to liberate women:

WOMEN'S LIBERATION. Throw away your belt and special panties — switch to new Freelife.

New products are launched, designed to appeal to the so-called 'new woman', one who is supposedly 'liberated'. She has her own job and an income of her own, so she becomes yet another area of the market to exploit:

You've come a long way, baby!
Virginia Slims advertisement

As far as advertising goes the only freedom presented as worth having is just the freedom to spend — to buy, buy, buy.

Women's efforts at getting the attention of men often lead to competition between them. They are also noted for being more 'bitchy' than men as a result.
It is because of men that women dislike each other.
The most divisive factor between women is competition between women for men.

How much truth do you think there is in these statements? How important is it for your girlfriend to look good? Do you expect her to take more trouble than you do over her appearance?

Do you know anyone who has had **anorexia nervosa** or has taken dieting to great extremes? How did they behave?

3
WHAT A DRAG
IT IS GETTING OLD

When you see an old man you should sit down and take a lesson;
when you see an old woman you should throw a stone.

> Afghan proverb

Women grow old. Men mature.

> Traditional saying

Keep young and beautiful if you want to be loved.

> Traditional saying

There is a normal dislike of getting old, and nobody, man or
woman, actually looks forward to it. Real old age, being in your
seventies and eighties, is generally an ordeal for both sexes.

I want to be young and stay young for a long, long time.

> — A television ad

But many of the trials surrounding **growing older** are ones
that women feel more than men. Women are actually ashamed
of growing older before they're anywhere near old age. In our
society a great deal of value is placed on being young, because
while you're young you're at your most productive. Also you
have more money to spend and can therefore buy and consume
more. Notice how little advertising is directed at people on
social security.

Once they've reached their mid twenties, women are generally reluctant to reveal how old they are. They often dislike having to state their age, whether it is on a routine form, a marriage license, a job application or when a policeman stops them for speeding. They may even lie about how old they are and nobody will think it strange. If a man lied about his age, however, he would be thought a little peculiar. It is thought to be bad manners to ask a woman her age, so the French have a polite way of putting it. For a woman between the age of twenty and sixty is regarded as being 'of a certain age'. This double standard about age hits women hard — like a car, the older the model the less it is worth. Growing older for the vast majority of women purely and simply means becoming less attractive.

Ageing in a woman is seen as making her not only unattractive but repulsive and almost obscene to the world. Sexually women are considered less desirable, which is reflected in their chances of marrying or remarrying after they are forty. Middle-aged men usually have very little trouble in finding a partner, often a lot younger than themselves. It is socially accepted that men be older than their wives — but less so the other way around. Notice just how often newspapers comment on the fact when an older woman marries a man younger than herself.

There is pressure on women to stay young-looking while men are allowed to age without being made conscious of it. Being physically attractive counts much more in life for women than for men. Being beautiful is associated with youthfulness, so there is a desperate fight to stave off any signs of ageing. The standard of beauty for an older woman is judged by how far she manages to look younger than she is. But what makes men unattractive to women has very little to do with their getting old. Their value as husbands and lovers is decided by what they do rather than what they look like. Fame, money, power — all make a man more sexually attractive, and these often increase with age. But they don't make a woman more attractive. What she has to do is to keep young.

Dear Liz:
My boyfriend says he would like to take me out with him but is
too embarrassed.
The trouble is that he is 32 and I am 45.
— A letter to the problem page of a magazine

Would you be embarrassed if you were the boyfriend?

Hugh Hefner on growing old:

**My 40s have been better than my 30s, which were fabu-
lous, and I expect my 50s to be even better than my 40s,
because until it actually starts to impair you physically,
ageing is largely a state of mind.**

Could this apply equally well to one of Hefner's Bunnies?

4
THE JUDGEMENT OF PARIS

In a Greek myth Paris had to choose the fairest of three goddesses. Juno promised him a kingdom; Minerva military
glory; while Venus offered him the fairest woman in the
world. Paris awarded Venus the golden apple. In return he got
Helen of Troy . . .

A few thousand years later men are still judging women on their
looks. Not only are women looked up and down and assessed in
the street and in ordinary everyday life, at interviews for jobs,
but we even arrange competitions for the purpose. And if you're
female, you have the chance to have your looks judged from
childhood to middle age, to be a Miss Pears Soap or the Glamorous Granny at a holiday resort. The ultimate event in Europe
is the Miss World contest. Some would call it a prize cattle
market. In America we go even further and decide on a Miss
Universe.

Venus got an apple, but if you're Miss World what is the prize?
Well, if you are a fourth it's $500 — a sum that would hardly
cover your expenses. For the winner it is $2,300 and a year's
world tour. But not sightseeing — it's hard work, with Miss
World publicizing and promoting products every step of the
way. But she's making money — for others.

While she is being judged the whole nation is watching the
spectacle on television. But before this, the bookmakers have
been taking bets as to the outcome. As an event it is the human
equivalent of the World Series.

The judges reach their final decision on the basis of what the
girls look like. To this end the contestants are required to pa-
rade on and off stage three times in different outfits. In national
costume (or an attempt at it), in evening dress and finally, if
they have managed to get that far, in a bathing suit for the final
heat. The contestants actually get to talk for about a minute,
but only if they're one of the lucky seven finalists. This is

96

supposedly their chance to prove that they've got not only looks to their credit, but intelligence, charm and personality as well: 'What does your boyfriend think of all this?', or 'Did you make your own dress?' Some of the questions are almost an insult to the intelligence. So one year there was a effort to ask supposedly 'intellectual' questions. 'Do you think this country is on its way to spiritual decline and moral Armaggedon?', or 'Do you think the great natural resources of your country will ever be exhausted?', or 'Who is your favorite 18th-century novelist?'

Since these questions were unexpected, and the contestants had about ten seconds to answer, it's not surprising that most of them looked a little stunned.

But if you thought Miss World contestants were judged solely on looks and personality you're sadly mistaken. The 1974 Miss World gave up her title within forty-eight hours because of the rumors and disapproval that surrounded her private life.

MAN'S WORLD

Would anyone give a damn if the strongest man in the world turned out to be an unmarried father five times over and involved in half a dozen divorce suits?

Helen Morgan's only 'crime' is that she is a woman and in today's society, where double standards are still the norm, that's fatal.

Letter to a newspaper

Even before the development of the women's movement, many women felt angry and indignant about beauty contests. In September 1968 a group demonstrated at the Miss America Pageant in Atlantic City. They threw high heeled shoes, girdles, bras and other things into trash cans, to symbolize both their freedom from uncomfortable sex-typed clothing and their feelings that beauty aids are really garbage. Afterwards, members of the women's movement were labelled 'bra burners', although nobody there burned a bra.

The Miss America contest has been described as degrading to women. What is your judgement?
Do you ever think of beauty contestants as men?
What qualities do you need to be Mr. Universe?

5
MAGAZINES TO SUIT YOU

On any newsagent's stand there is a dazzling selection of magazines. Have you noticed that most of these are aimed at one sex or the other? Since men's and women's interests are separate on the whole, the magazines that people buy reflect this separation.

Men's magazines like *High Fidelity* tend to provide detailed and factual information about men's hobbies. They assume that the men who read them have considerable technical competence, that they understand scientific terms and derive pleasure and satisfaction from making and building complicated things. The reader is assumed to be a 'he'.

The corresponding women's magazines that deal with hobbies, such as *Sphere,* are usually about crafts. They tend to treat their subject in more human terms. Women develop skills not just as hobbies for themselves, but also to make their homes more attractive and give pleasure to their friends and families.

Both types of magazine reflect the regrettable separation of skills and hobbies between the sexes.

There is, however, one range of magazines exclusively for women, which has no equivalent for men. These are the women's magazines, covering romance, fashion and beauty for every age group. Girls can progress from *Seventeen,* then to the young fashion magazines like *Mademoiselle,* and later to *Cosmopolitan* or *Good Housekeeping,* among others. The differences between what the two sexes read are quite startling, as shown in the following comments by a group of teenagers.

What I read and why

Girls talking

I like reading romantic stories because mostly they are sad, sweet and loving and I like crying. They are about schoolgirl love — Him and Me. They always have a happy ending.

I like *Seventeen* because there are quizzes to do, like: Are you vain? What looks nice on you, what do people think of you? I also like the fashion and beauty.

I started to read *Photoplay* when David Cassidy became famous — I would always look to see if there was something on him, and there usually was.

I read *Woman's Day* magazine because I love to look out for recipes, tips for dressmaking and how to change old things into new.

Boys talking

I read *Road and Track* magazine. It is about the world's fastest machines like racing cars and motorbikes. There are many interesting things like illustrations and diagrams of how a machine works and is made. It teaches me a lot about electronics and technology.

I like to read *Spiderman* because it is very adventurous. It makes you think that if you were the Hulk, Spiderman etc. you would feel really great.

The reason I buy *Sports Illustrated* is that it has all the latest and important news about football.

I get *Creem* every month, because you can find out about the latest records, and I enjoy the interviews they have with the different musicians.

For the carefree girl

Let's look at one of the leading 'fashion magazines', aimed at the single girl who wants to make sure she is having a good time. The overall image is of action and excitement — everything is happening to people who read this magazine, so if *you* read it, it will happen to you too. Advertisements take up a very large amount of space, so it becomes hard to tell what is an article and what's an ad.

If a girl wants to look fashionable she really has to buy a magazine, to guide her in her buying.

Our image is of a sophisticated young magazine. We try to include all the issues that concern young people. For they are the people that will be involved in the future with problems like ecology and test-tube babies. It used to be all sex and boyfriends, but now the attitudes of young people are changing. Our best articles have been those that actually got something done; for example we did an expose of the rag trade, and another on model agencies.

Magazine editor

It is remarkable that these two 'best articles' were both about the world of fashion.

There is lots of news about entertainment, pop and film stars, but very little on anything more serious, as that might be too taxing for girls who buy a magazine for 'fashion and fun'. It would be an intrusion to make them think about their lives.

We would not have articles on politics . . . but we might do something on an interesting personality. We would never try to interfere in our readers' personal lives — so we don't carry articles on personal relationships . . . We always give both sides to an argument, maybe two people both giving their point of view. For example, we did this on the subject of virginity. Since it's impossible to be unbiased about Women's Lib we decided to leave it out!

Magazine editor

101

The information a girl gets from her magazines is certainly not the hard, technical stuff that a boy expects from his, so that he can do something constructive, like take a motorbike apart or build a speedboat.
And for the future?
We will be catering for the homey side of girls. They are now showing more interest in making homes, getting married and buying goods for the home.

Editor

A world of one's own

The subjects that women are involved with and interested in are dealt with in the magazines for them. This is usually an extremely restricted list — childbirth and childcare, cookery, knitting, home decorating, and so forth. It's an interesting reflection of the changes in attitudes towards women, and their changing attitudes towards themselves, that the leading magazines in this area — *McCall's, Journal* and *Good Housekeeping* — have had to expand the range of subjects covered. Now some issues not previously considered to be of interest to women are examined. One of them even has a problem page for men, which raises an important question: why are issues such as abortion and contraception, emotional and marriage problems and childcare seen only as women's concern? Surely men should be thinking about them too? And the fact that men actually do write in to a problem page in a women's magazine, and that many men admit to reading and enjoying these magazines, shows that these are areas of concern to both sexes and should no longer be confined to women alone.

But still most of these 'women's magazines' stick to the idea of keeping the roles of women and men separate. And certainly even the more forward-looking ones could go much further, with more articles on politics, the economy and all those other areas that are assumed to interest only men.

For the past five years a new magazine for women, called *Ms*, has been on the market. It is published by members of the women's liberation movement and offers the first mass market

102

alternative to the usual type of women's magazine. It makes a serious attempt to look at our lives in an honest way, and to talk about important things in women's lives directly. There are many other, smaller alternative magazines and newspapers for women. Some are listed in the back of this book.

Look at a copy of a hi-fi, photographic or motorcycle magazine. Which sex are the readers assumed to be?
Do girls ever make hi-fis, take photographs or ride motorcycles? Do you think men ever buy *Redbook* or *Woman's Day*? Do you think they would be embarrassed to buy it for themselves? What magazines do you and your friends read? What do you like most about them? Is there anything you would criticize in them? Draw up a plan for a unisex magazine that would appeal equally to both sexes. What sort of material would you have to put in it, so that neither sex would feel it wasn't for them?
Get hold of a copy of the magazine *Ms*. Compare what's in it with the kinds of magazines we've discussed.

The waves lashed against the shore — escapist fiction

Women by and large are the market for romantic fiction — whether serialized in magazines or borrowed from the library. When young they dream romance will happen to them, and when older they indulge in romantic dreams that real life and real marriage have not always fulfilled.

The plots in these stories are very similar, and tend to follow one of the following patterns:
(1) girl meets boy and they fall in love;
(b) girl strays from nice boy to go after scoundrel, but sees the error of her ways, and comes back to nice boy;
(c) girl who runs around learns the error of her ways, then starts to search for 'true love' as all girls should.
The last is the least common pattern because it doesn't have the happy ending of a big kiss and declaration of love for her. Endings are very important in these stories — for they always explain past misunderstandings and promise future happiness:

103

Oh Jenny darling, it was always you I really loved.

Look at a magazine like *Redbook* for examples of stories that follow along these lines.

There are other stories where, for example, a girl's dull working week is completely transformed just by a boy's smile.

The smile made her feel as though she were going down a lift, very fast.

What incredible facial muscles he must have had! Or the girl who meets her love because of her dog:

Look Helen, that first day in the park, I just used Snoopy as an excuse to get talking to you.

In romantic stories the first contact with the man, especially the kiss or embrase, completely transforms the woman — she loses all her senses and experiences apparent ecstasy:

As Paul's arms came around me and his lips found mine, I felt as if I had stepped back in time. My husband, my daughter — everything was blotted out of my mind. I was the same girl I'd been six years ago . . .

She's likely to forget under these circumstances that she is married to someone else, and she always knows at this moment that this is 'real' love.

There is always a sense of great desperation in these stories, as though what happens and making the right, vital decision are matters of life and death.

Two women in my life and they both needed me in totally different ways. Dear God, I thought desperately, how much longer could I — could we all — go on like this?

The men are usually rugged surly types, distant loners who drift into a small town, understood by nobody. These types leave nothing but memories and broken hearts behind them (unless

104

they meet the right girl, who changes them — and their love is therefore permanent).

'Forget him, Claire,' Sue kept begging me. 'He's a drifter. We all warned you before he went away!' How could she understand that Don would always be with me — in my heart?

Notice too that women are always either looking for, or falling in and out of, love. The course of events seems to be guided by some force of destiny — things just happen if they are going to, and the women have no control over their lives and futures. And notice that 'love' is seen as a sensation in the stomach, something that the woman can spot immediately as 'real' and that she experiences only *once.*

Do you think this is like real life?
What part does physical sex play in these stories?
Why do you think this kind of writing holds much less appeal for men?

6
AND NOW FOR SOMETHING COMPLETELY DIFFERENT

. . . For him

We've looked at some of the most popular magazines for women, dealing with their 'special interests'. One of the best selling 'special interests' for men are the girlie magazines, one of which is *Playboy,* started by Hugh Hefner.

The master ponce of Western Society is Hugh Hefner, who invented brothels where the whores are only to be looked at, which are brothels just the same.
Germaine Greer, *The Female Eunuch, Paladin,* 1971

Hefner is most famous for being the originator of *Playboy* magazine and for being the brain behind the 'bunnies', but as he said in *Playboy* magazine:

Did you know that I almost called the magazine 'Stag Party' and the symbol was originally going to be a stag? I changed my mind just before we went to press, thank God. Somehow, it wouldn't have been the same. Can you imagine a chain of key clubs staffed by beautiful girls wearing antlers?

The answer to that is, of course, yes. If it would make a profit, then the 'beautiful girls' *would* be wearing them. It's a debatable question as to which is the more ridiculous, wearing antlers or wearing floppy rabbit ears. A rabbit is, however, a lot more cuddly than a stag. Try and imagine a man wearing either for a living!

Playboy magazine is famous for its pinup pictures of big-breasted young women. As Hefner says himself, 'Well, I can't deny that I prefer big ones to small ones . . . My taste in women isn't exactly a personal aberration; it happens to be shared with some 26,000,000 *Playboy* readers' who are, as he goes on to say, 'no different in this regard from the overshelming majority of the male population of the world.' So ask yourself if you, or the rest of the female population, come up to *Playboy* standards: young, beautiful, with big breasts?

If most of the world's population agree with Hugh Hefner, what effect is this likely to have on women themselves?

Even a relatively sophisticated magazine as 'Newsweek' has criticized 'Playboy' for marring its otherwise excellent editorial content with what is termed a 'peek-a-boo' interest in sex; but as far as I'm concerned, incorporating the two is 'Playboy's' greatest virtue.

Hefner

How do you think *Playboy,* and magazines of that genre, make their money? Is it by
(a) producing a thought-provoking magazine?
(b) selling sex in an acceptable way?
Would the readers and purchasers of *Playboy* continue to buy the magazine if there were no pictures of naked women in it?

The girls who model for *Playboy* are, Hefner claims, chosen from everyday life — they're not 'aloof movie queens or professional models' — but he admits that his team have to 'scour the country' to find them. It's also been suggested that the pictures themselves are retouched and air-sprayed to remove the slightest imperfections on the model — so that the finished article is perfect.

Would the magazine sell as well if head-and-shoulder portraits were shown? As one subscriber admitted, 'I suppose I might buy the mag without pinups — but I guess I'm the exception.'

Paul Raymond talking . . .

Paul Raymond runs a similar magazine in England called *Men Only*. Here is his opinion of his magazine.

(Q.) Can you briefly outline what you believe the public wants from a men's magazine?
(Raymond) I think that they want to be entertained, it's as simple as that.
(Q.) What is your formula for entertainment?
(Raymond)*Nude birds* of course, various articles which would include ones on sex and also a few non-sexual articles as well.

This seems to be the formula for the success of men's magazines in general.

The pinups of women, along with the products advertised and the humor, are offered to men for entertainment, enjoyment and consumption along with food, wine and cigarettes.

In order to achieve the image of their ideal selves as presented by magazines, both men and women are told to spend money and to follow a particular life-style — they're both exploited by advertisements. But in this process, women themselves become products, which have to be worked at and perfected, while men are basically the consumers who buy, select and possess.

. . . For her

A rather silly attempt at 'instant Women's Lib' was the launching of a magazine similar to *Playboy* — called *Playgirl*. The idea was that if men could have pinups, then so could women, but funnily enough, most women don't find the naked men in the magazine either attractive or sexy — the usual reaction is shrieks of laughter. Partly this may be because the men don't pose in sexy positions . . . they're either awkwardly and aimlessly standing by a tree, or pictured by the dozen as a football team. But it may also be because it's only recently been regarded as possible for women to be active and to show an open interest in sex. Women are used to seeing themselves in a passive role — their bodies are to be looked at by men for their pleasure and stimulation. But they're not used to seeing men's bodies for that same purpose. Therefore naked, posing men are sometimes rather strange to the eye: women aren't used to finding them erotic or beautiful.

If you looked at 'girlie' magazines, would you do it out of interest or 'for a laugh' with your friends? Would the subject ever embarrass you? If so, why?

7
NUDES OF THE WORLD

'Buy me . . . fly me . . .'

Advertisers have found that one very good method of selling a product is to have a woman next to it — usually naked. It adds instant glamor, particularly if it's aimed at men. The message is often that if the man buys the goods he will attract a beautiful girl — a persuasive idea. There is almost the suggestion that the girl comes along with the goods as part of the deal, or at least this feeds his imagination enough to make him consider buying the product. Sometimes the item being advertised is so unrelated to a naked woman's body that to see them side by side is laughable, but it's often effective advertising.

One very common example is in the advertisements for airlines. They rarely mention the efficiency of the aircraft or the skill of the pilot. What is 'sold' to the businessman who uses the airline is the soft-voiced, sexy stewardess who will make his journey comfortable. She may simply invite him enticingly: 'I'm Jo, fly me.'

Holiday brochures are another example. But here the girls aren't offering a service themselves — the suggestion is that if you take this holiday, you'll meet girls like this, so it must be a good place. And if women go on the holiday this warns them of the kind of opposition they will have to compete with. The message may be put over simply by a picture of a girl in a bikini in front of the swimming pool, or it may be accompanied by a message implying that the girl and the holiday go together.

A man's most prized possession is usually his car, so when these are advertised there is often a woman either in it or on it. She's telling men in no uncertain terms that if they buy this car they'll without doubt acquire their next most important possession — a beautiful woman, or women. There is often a whole crowd of admiring beauties gasping with delight at the man's wonderful machine.

One year, naked women were actually used to adorn cars at the London Motor Show, but 'public decency' was so outraged that the policy was abandoned.

If a man is relying on his looks and body alone to attract women, he's a good target for the after-shave advertisements. These usually depict only a woman who declares that there's only one sort of man she could go for — the one that uses X after-shave and talc. She'll attack him wildly in public, sent crazy by his smell. A little exaggerated, you may think — and not to be taken seriously — but it has made the man think about his image just enough to remember to buy the product:

For the Man who gets what he wants — Rogue Toiletries

Even the family do-it-yourself man is not safe from the snare. If he's looking out for storm windows, paint, bathroom fixtures or a central air conditioner, he's likely to be caught by the sight of the naked woman, whom he can at least *imagine* living in his house once it is improved by this product. Women are even used to drive power mowers — half-naked, of course — and to work power drills, in low-necked dresses: all to get the men interested.

Men are very much exploited by these advertisements. But in exploiting men, women themselves are degraded by making the female body into something completely passive, making sex the guarantee of quality.

In one normal week, count the number of times you see naked or near-naked women used in advertising, such as on paperback covers and outside cinemas. Do you think this does any harm to anybody? Do you see naked men as often?

Glossary . . . What do they mean by?

AUTONOMY — a state of mind where someone makes his/her own choices.

CHAUVINISM — an excessive attachment or bias to the group or place to which one belongs. A male chauvinist is someone who believes, or acts as if he believes, in the superiority of male over female.

CONDITION — to adapt, modify or mold so as to conform to the society or culture one is in.

CONSCIOUSNESS-RAISING — the change of someone's awareness of the world and the way they are affected by it — achieved through experience and discussion with others.

EXPLOITATION — an unjust or improper use of another person for someone's own profit or advantage.

FEMINISM — the theory of political, social and economic equality of the sexes. Also, organized activity on behalf of the rights and interests of women.

FEMINIST — someone who supports the liberation of women.

GENDER — loosely, it means one's sex.

IMAGE — an image is a mental picture of something not actually present. It also means a mental idea held in common by members of a group, and is symbolic of their shared attitude and approach.

LIBERATION — the act of setting free.

MATRIARCHY — a system of social organization in which the woman is the head of the family.

MISOGYNIST — a man who shows hatred or distrust of women. The equivalent word for a woman who hates men is a man-hater!

OPPRESSION — the unjust or cruel exercise of authority or power, or the sense of being weighed down in body and mind.

PATRIARCHY — social organization in which the father is the head of the clan or family, wives and children are legally dependent on the male, and descent and inheritance are usually through the male line.

SEXISM — prejudice and discrimination against people on the grounds of their sex (cf. racism and classism). In our society, usually refers to prejudice against women.

SEX ROLE — a particular way of acting and behaving which society expects of you because of your sex.
STEREOTYPE — something conforming to a fixed or general picture that is held in common by members of a group. A stereotype represents an oversimplified opinion or emotional attitude, or an uncritical judgement.

POSTSCRIPT

We'd like to think that reading this book, and the two others in the series, has made you think about things in a way you hadn't before; we hope they will make you question the way things happen to you, and help you to make good choices in your own lives.

C.A. and R.L.

FOLLOW UP
AND BIBLIOGRAPHY

If you are interested in finding out more about any of the issues raised in this book, the following sources may be useful: National Organization for Women. The NOW Action Center, 425 13th Street N.W., Suite 1001, Washington D.C. 20004 will provide information over the telephone or by mail about the organization and its activities. Local chapters may be listed in your telephone directory.
First Things First, 23 7th Street S.E., Washington, D.C. 20003 is a distributor of women's liberation materials: write for their catalog.

Here is a very short list of women's periodicals that may interest you:

Bibliography:

Off Our Backs, 1724 20th Street N.W., Washington, D.C. 20009
Majority Report, 74 Grove Street, New York, New York 10014
Sister, P.O. Box 3438 Yale Station, New Haven, Conn. 06520
Maine Freewoman's Herald, 193 Middle Street, Portland,
   Maine 04111
Her-Self, 225 East Liberty Street, Ann Arbor, Michigan 48108
Big Mama Rag, 1724 Gaylord Street, Denver, Colorado 80208
Union W.A.G.E., P.O. Box 462, Berkeley, California 94701
Sister, P.O. Box 597, Venice, California 90291
Pandora, Box 94, Seattle, Washington 98105

Further information and useful addresses can be found in *New Women's Survival Sourcebook*, by Susan Rennie and Kirsten Grimstad, Knopf, 1975. A comprehensive bibliography is in Sheila Rowbotham, *Women, Resistance and Revolution*, Vintage, 1973.

Of general interest:
Carol Adams and Rae Laurikietis, *The Gender Trap*, Academy Press, 1977. Book 1: Education and Work; Book 2: Sex and Marriage.
Simone de Beauvoir, *The Second Sex*, Vintage, 1974.
Betty Friedan, *The Feminine Mystique*, Dell, 1975.
Hannah Gavron, *The Captive Wife*, Penguin, 1969 (Humanities, 1966).
Germaine Greer, *The Female Eunuch*, Bantam, 1972.
Kate Millet, *Sexual Politics*, Avon, 1971.
Juliet Mitchell, *Women's Estate*, Vintage, 1973.
Elaine Morgan, *The Descent of Woman*, Bantam, 1973.
Robin Morgan (Ed.), *Sisterhood is Powerful*, Vintage, 1970.
Sheila Rowbotham, *Woman's Consciousness, Man's World*, Penguin, 1974.
Fay Weldon, *Down Among the Women*, Warner, 1974.
Virginia Woolf, *A Room of One's Own*, Harcourt Brace, 1963.

Particularly relevant to this book are:
Aphra, Lincoln Sq. Community Council Center for the Arts. 150 West 68, N.Y., N.Y. 10023. The oldest feminist literary quarterly.
Feminist Writers' Workshop, *The Feminist English Dictionary*, vol. I, 1973. (Available from YWCA of Chicago, 37 South Wabash, Chicago, IL 60637.)
Molly Haskell, *From Reverence to Rape: the Treatment of Women in the Movies*, Penguin, 1974.
Casey Miller and Kate Swift, *Words and Women*. Doubleday, 1976.
Ms Magazine. At your newsstand.

Organizations of Interest
Clearing House on Women's Studies, The Feminist Press, Box 334, Old Westbury, New York. Publishes a directory of women's studies programs in the United States; write for their catalog.
The Grey Panthers, 3700 Chestnut Street, Philadelphia, PA 19104. Maggie Kuhn, an active feminist in her seventies, founded this group to combat ageism.
Know, Inc. Box 86031, Pittsburgh, PA 15221. Feminist publishers and distributors with a large stock of posters, records, reports, offprints and hard to find movement literature.
New Day Films, P.O. Box 315, Franklin Lakes, New Jersey 07417. Distributors of women's films.
Women in Distribution, P.O. Box 8858, Washington, D.C. 20003 Feminist books and records.
Women's Institute for Freedom of the Press, 3306 Ross Place, N.W., Washington, D.C. 20008. Holds seminars, gives advice; publishes *Media Report to Women,* free to women in media.

Films made by women:
Look out for films made by women. The following are a few of the best-known women writers and directors and their films, but there are many more. These are not necessarily their best films, but ones you may be able to see:
Dorothy Arzner, *Dance Girl Dance* (USA, 1940)
Nelly Kaplan, *A Very Curious Dance* (France, 1969)
Barbara Loeden, *Wanda* (USA, 1970)
Ida Lupino, *The Bigamist* (USA, 1953)
Leni Riefenstahl, *The Triumph of the Will* (Germany, 1936)
Leontine Sagan, *Maedchen in Uniform* (Germany, 1931)
Agnes Varda, *Cleo from 5 to 7* (France, 1967)
Lina Wertmuller, *The Lizards* (Italy, 1963)